KU-202-671

Contents

BOOST YOUR CREATIVE INTELLIGENCE

Harry Alder

KOGAN PAGE AG

First published in 2002 entitled CQ: *Boost Your Creative Intelligence*
Reissued in 2005 entitled *Boost Your Creative Intelligence*

Kogan Page Ltd
120 Pentonville Road
London N1 9JN
www.kogan-page.co.uk

© Harry Alder, 2002

British Library Cataloguing in Publication Data

A CIP record for this book is available from the British Library

ISBN 0 7494 3706 5

Typeset by Saxon Graphics Ltd, Derby
Printed and bound in Great Britain by Clays Ltd, St Ives plc

Preface

This book approaches creativity from two perspectives that are rarely mixed, and that I have not to date combined. It draws on the latest scientific research, and differentiates between scientific findings and what I term folklore – the standard self-help and how-to format into which most popular books on creativity fall, including several of my own. The latter is the popular approach in which the author's word goes, and if it doesn't, you will have a job finding chapter and verse to prove otherwise. But such a book is 'accessible', as publishers like to say, and easy reading for a person of average intelligence, and with little or no previous knowledge on the subject.

My aim has been to reconcile these two approaches. That meant omitting the academic trappings and the worst of the jargon whilst avoiding dumbing down but incorporating recent research. I have spared you the discontinuity of multiple references, footnotes, endnotes and citations that usually adorn a scholarly treatment. However, I refer to the main writers and researchers in the narrative so you will know the ultimate source of anything implied as gospel, and can explore further anything of particular interest. Checking out information is so much easier than it used to be, thanks to the Internet and World Wide Web, and most readers who need to dig deeper will have the know-how to do that. My use of the shorthand 'CQ' will not satisfy the academic purists but I have had to live with their

120-plus definitions of creativity and its characteristics for long enough. A seamless hybrid is a tall order and I lapse in places into either heavyweight technical background or featherweight populist prose. But I hope that on balance the book meets the needs of 'thinking' readers. As far as readability is concerned, and allowing for the odd technical bits, I hope you will not see the join.

I imagine that Stephen Hawking set out to steer such a middle route in his latest book on the cosmos, *The Universe in a Nutshell*. That was after finding that very few people managed to get to the end of his memorable book *A Brief History of Time*, even though he wrote it specifically for popular consumption – and consumed it was, at the bookshop level. Unfortunately, whilst I could understand the words and sentences he used, I couldn't begin to grasp the concepts that he seemed to take for granted, such as extra dimensions and parallel universes. I hoped that my subject would not stretch the mind as much. However, Hawking himself acknowledges the human brain as the most complex thing we can ever try to understand, and creativity lies somewhere in the particularly incomprehensible corners of that super organ. Nevertheless, I did get a sense of the awesome wonder of the outer universe, as I do in learning more about human creativity closer to home. I could not work out, however, how understanding a black hole helped me to raise a family, pay bills and do well at work. I am more optimistic about creativity. Readers' expectations vary, but we can usually put creativity to work immediately in our personal lives – the literature confirms that creativity is not confined to the Einsteins and Hawkings. Even the scantiest understanding of what the brain can do and the particular way it does it can turn an ordinary life around.

Electricity – and any invisible wavy things – are, to me, no easier to really understand than quasars, quarks and 'branes' (or is that just spelling?). But I can learn a lot about how it is made and delivered to my house and see its magic displayed by the press of a switch. Human creativity is magic of cosmic proportions which some say we will never fully understand – something about the pot second-guessing the potter. But more importantly for most of us, and the reason for this book, you can harness your innate creativity for specific and important purposes, with some pleasant surprises thrown in.

Introduction

The German poet Schiller used to write with his feet in ice water. Other poets relied on the Muse. Schiller, although he probably didn't realize it, increased the blood flow to his brain, which, it seems, made it work better. Einstein took imaginary galactic cheap day returns on light beams. Fertile imaginations and against-the-flow creative thinking have given us science, art and civilization.

We are not too clear about just what makes a person creative, or even what creativity is, but most people know it when they see it. What we see are 'brainwaves' and the 'aha', eureka-type flashes of inspiration we get from time to time. These delightful experiences are the bubbles that come to the surface.

We may know it when we see it, but we don't always see it, or at least do not attribute it to creative thinking. For instance, highly creative people clock up all sorts of personal achievements that they and others do not relate to their particular, creative way of thinking. Put another way, we universally underrate the god-like power of the human mind – even of a five-year-old. If it were possible to trace the origin of every artifice around us I doubt whether many would have arisen without what we think of as creative thinking – insights, intuition, leaps of logic, or just the product of an unfettered imagination. Were they to tell their stories, bridges, buildings, carpets, light bulbs and mattresses, for example, would probably all trace their ancestry to creative bubbles. Even the laws and principles on which modern science is based were more than likely to have been conceived in moments of creative insight, rather than by ordered reasoning.

One of the tests of true creativity is how quickly we take ideas and inventions for granted and imagine that anyone could have thought of that. The wheel was a great idea, but using *four* – hardly in the top 'eureka' league – has also turned out to be rather useful. Because we see life in hindsight we miss the magic moments. Usefulness, or 'appropriateness', it so happens, is one of the classical criteria of creativity we will meet in the book.

What with mad artists and the like, historically creativity has sometimes had a bad press. The left hand (left = Latin *sinister*) has always had iffy connotations and is connected to the right brain with its own, mute, other-world associations. This misunderstood cranial cauldron of creativity has yet to emerge into the modern world of science. The 60-something wildly differing definitions of creativity in the literature don't help its shaky scientific credentials. Straight, no-tricks-or-surprises logical thinking that you can model on a desk computer is easier for most researchers to swallow.

There is none the less no doubt about the enormous contribution that creative people have made to art, science and civilization even if we can't name them all or trace their creativity to moments of inspiration. Yet only a handful of famous people have been recognized for their special creativity. History has credited other factors for success in government, business, sport, education and other spheres of life. The same applies today: we don't appreciate the contribution individual creative thinkers have made to so much of the man-made world we take for granted.

Creativity quotient

Reference to eminent creative people confirms the wide degree of creativity from person to person, and between children and adults. I have used the term CQ – the Q standing for quotient, as in emotional quotient (EQ) and intelligence quotient (IQ), or 'quality', as creativity is a *qualitative* characteristic. IQ is a *quantitative* measure, being expressed in numbers with 100 as the average. EQ is also a qualitative measure, and psychometric instruments that put numbers to it are not standardized or validated and therefore of little use to anyone. EQ is a shorthand way of expressing the relative qualitative measure of the different factors that it embraces – mainly self-knowledge and people skills, or 'intrapersonal intelligence' and 'interpersonal intelligence'. CQ is a shorthand way of expressing the qualitative measure of the main components of creativity.

Some of these creativity factors are well known and are incorporated in tests used around the world (Chapter 11 addresses creativity psychometrics). They mainly comprise what is known as divergent thinking, and, like intelligence measures, do not tell the whole story. We shall see in Chapter 2 on definitions that there is no agreement on what creativity is, so it cannot be quantified in numbers anyway. However, just as we all think we can spot an intelligent person, we know intuitively when we meet with creativity in people. This can be a footballer or Formula 1 racing driver as well as a performing artist, entrepreneur or scientist – or just an 'ideas' person. 'She's got a high CQ' reflects this overall evaluation of creativity rather than any specific aspects as included in a questionnaire. The important thing for us is that we can *increase* our CQ in many ways. We are not stuck with a genetic ration. Even more limited concepts like IQ are moveable by several percentage points, as I show in my book *Boost Your Intelligence* (Kogan Page). But when it comes to CQ, as a package of different personal traits and processes, it is feasible to double it and thus experience a far greater impact on your life.

Some people get half a dozen ideas before breakfast and a few more spread throughout the day. They put down the origin of most of their successes in life to spontaneous creative insights, or flashes of inspiration. Likewise the experience of 'flow' or being 'in the zone' (Chapter 5), which nearly everyone experiences from time to time, can become a frequent, exhilarating and maybe everyday part of a person's life. These are ordinary people I meet on training courses around the world who have cottoned on to using their brain in a better way. They are not latter-day Einsteins and every one of us can learn from them and from decades of research on what makes a person creative.

Regardless of numbers, you *know* when your CQ is increasing. You can *count* 'eureka' and 'flow' experiences and even grade them for quality or dollar value. Or simply trace creative insights to a more fulfilling job, a personal achievement in your chosen hobby, a better home environment, a loving wife or husband or a new sense of self-confidence in everything you put your hand to. So a substantial increase in CQ is possible if you are serious about harnessing your innate creativity.

Big C creativity

Creativity is bigger than ever today, as Chapter 1 outlines, and extraordinary claims have been made about its role in shaping the 21st century. That's on a global basis, but the biggest impact will be in the lives of ordinary people who begin to think in a better way.

Human creativity is a topic that has been pondered for centuries but with little agreement as to definition, as we shall see in Chapter 2. But some of the important facts, based not least on improved brain-scanning technology, have just become known in recent years. Recent advances in our understanding of how the mind works have helped to explain human achievement that we would otherwise have put down to innate talent, sheer hard work or serendipity. Importantly for most of us, we have confirmed that extraordinary creativity is possible with a standard-issue brain. Chapter 3 addresses the central role of the brain. Better still – and this is what the book is about – you can learn to stimulate and harness your innate creativity to make your personal world better.

This is not a book about creativity techniques. They are fine for creative people who in the main buy the books, so it is all a bit self-fulfilling. The sort of creativity we all aspire to comes from somewhere very deep in the labyrinth of the mind where our beliefs, attitudes and motivations lie. Creativity means far more than formulae and techniques.

Thankfully, with parallel advances in psychology and neuro-linguistic programming, as well as computer-enhanced scanning, these regions of the mind are no longer out of bounds. We can identify and change the most ingrained, long-term traits that play a part in our creativity and everything else that makes us unique individuals. Based on scientific research for half a century, but mainly in the past decade or so, we can identify which critical traits need to be revived or fine-tuned to produce the sort of creative outcomes we want. As we shall see in Chapter 4, we can learn a lot from people we know to be creative. We don't need to emulate great genetic talents, but simple thinking styles and attitudes that will make anyone more creative. For example, motivation is a key factor, which we address later in the book in Chapter 10.

People, processes and products

As well as learning from creative people we can learn from the creative processes they adopt, whether knowingly or unknowingly. Processes have been observed during actual creative spells, and we can learn how to personally harness and direct them to what is most important in our lives. Creative processes are covered in Chapter 5, which includes the well-known experience of 'flow' or being 'in the zone'.

Creativity is more than imagining and dreaming. Over a period truly creative people have something worthwhile to show for it, and in Chapter 6 we cover what is called the creative 'product'. By translating inspiration and ideas into worthwhile benefits we have something we can measure a little more easily than the internal workings of the mind. Creativity, we shall see, is best evaluated for its quality rather than quantity. So the Q in CQ can refer to both quality and 'quotient', as in intelligence quotient (IQ). The often-controversial link between intelligence and creativity is covered in Chapter 7.

None of this happens in a vacuum, and the people around you will have a say in who is a creative person and what is a creative product. Chapter 8 addresses the environment or 'system' within which we all exercise our creativity and its influence on what we produce. Chapter 9 describes a specific aspect of the creative environment – the important part that our own and other *cultures* play in what it means to be creative. This is rarely brought into the creativity equation so to some extent including a whole chapter redresses the balance.

All this means getting to know what creativity is all about and acquiring some of the simple but essential skills that highly creative people don't have to think about but most of us do. With the right information and know-how the techniques then start to make sense and work. For example, in Chapter 11 we cover the important question of creativity measurement, and the role of psychometrics, and in Chapter 12 some specific contributions to our understanding from scientific experimental work. Like the chapter on the influence of culture, this will help redress the balance and show where creativity has got to in a scientific sense. Chapter 13 addresses creativity in a business environment, and how to reconcile personal creativity with the needs and constraints of an inanimate organization.

The wider your knowledge about creativity the less you will depend on techniques and formulae and the more you will be able to draw on your own, unlimited resources. With a better all-round understanding of personal creative traits, processes and products you can start to live more creatively moment-by-moment rather than just at special, all-too-rare times. It will also provide a solid foundation for the skills you will apply to make mental changes where they are needed. That's when things start to 'flow' and extraordinary results happen.

CQ booster programme

Techniques have their place, and some apply to general conditioning skills rather than to specific tasks or problem solving. These are covered in Chapter 14, which also describes a number of popular task-related techniques. On the foundation of the knowledge you will gain from the book and in conjunction with the conditioning skills I describe, techniques – some of which you may be familiar with – will start to take on far more value. Chapter 14 summarizes the main lessons from the book and includes tips, techniques and lifestyle conditioning to form a personal programme for boosting your CQ. By then you will be familiar with the characteristics of creative people, the processes of creative thinking, the creative products you can expect to realize in your life and the outside influences on your creativity.

High creativity, with results to show for it, is a feasible project for people of average intelligence. You will draw on neural potential that already exists rather than waiting in hope for some elusive gift from outside. That means creativity is within your control. It is largely a *relearning* process – whether restoring self-belief or a boundless childhood imagination. Like reviving any lapsed habit (including bad ones), it can happen quickly. Best of all, the flow experience associated with human creativity is at the apex of pleasure and personal fulfilment, so it is an eminently worthwhile goal. Being blessed with a Mensa-level IQ (although the stuff of CVs) doesn't even compare. Creativity can be so much fun that it is worth taking seriously.

1

The big C

Creativity is big and getting bigger. It is widely seen as a legitimate subject for experimental science and has been recognized for its significance for organizations, cultures and global economic growth. True creativity is of incalculable value both to individuals and society. It has been argued that human creativity will be the most critical, scarce resource in the early decades of the third millennium. Society – some say – will divide into two categories: creatives, and the rest. Whatever creativity is, and whatever its impact will be in the coming years of endemic change, it is worth thinking about, and maybe getting a slice of the action.

The post-information age

The so-called information age has already made an impact that has changed all our lives. The purveyors of information for a short while during the closing decade or so of the twentieth century held the baton of power. The knowledge society; the information elite. But the growth of the Internet has *democratized* information. That means that the information that was said to contain such power will no longer reside in the hands of the privileged few. Quite the reverse has occurred. Some information will always have a special value, but much is now readily accessible, and – like any commodity – subject to universal laws of supply and demand. When you can download information from the Internet on just about any subject under the sun in minutes, its commercial value plummets.

Haves and have nots

Such an abundance of knowledge means we can all gain access to the modern-day equivalent of the library at Alexandria, cheaply and quickly, and with a standard brain. This includes all manner of technical information, such as is found in medical and legal textbooks and scientific research papers. We can access the combined archives of leading universities and national libraries for a small subscription and a local telephone call.

Futurists have talked of the information 'haves' and 'have-nots' as the new order in society. But if you don't mind learning the jargon you can acquire that 'scarce' resource without long, academic training. That levels the information playing fields. So what towards the close of the 20th century became for a while the scarce, critical resource, may no longer hold that position. That's in the nature of change, even at this heady, global level.

Brainpower

Brainpower, none the less, of one sort or another, will continue to be the key to a better future. The human brain is the most complex product of nature around, and there isn't an obvious competitor. It seems that 'the smart shall inherit the earth'. But what kind of brainpower? Not the sort of intelligence that stores, remembers and analyses information. Computers can perform such tasks better and faster than humans, so it hardly gives us the edge. This is not to undervalue such a mental function. In fact the sort of mathematical and logical intelligence we measure in IQ tests has historically been the most significant kind. For many years this ability to store and manipulate knowledge and get the 'right' answer has been the power behind our biggest political and commercial institutions – the only sort of brainpower recognized and valued. It even provided a blueprint for our ordered, hierarchical systems and structures. The logical, ordered brain sits as the supreme model of the 'organization'.

Cerebral donkey work

But surely not for long. We can delegate linear-type 'intelligence' to computers, and they beat us on memory speed. Even without computer power, we can reproduce this kind of 'intelligence' through a standardized educational system that faithfully transmits knowledge from teacher to student. Call it a 'replicable formula' or 'the McDonald's way' – effective machine-like 'intelligence', but essentially dumb. It doesn't break scientific barriers and contribute to human enlightenment. What used to appear as impressive feats of memory and analysis is now no more than number crunching, or cerebral donkey work. Most importantly, machine-like brain processing power does not *differentiate* the movers and shakers, the new millennial 'haves' and 'have nots'. Like anything that can be produced quickly with the help of machines, the ability to acquire, store and analyse information will become a commodity.

Happy surprises

Creative thinking is quite another story. History tells us that a different kind of brainpower produced the paradigm advances that have given us science, art and human civilization. We observe, for instance, sudden insights and extraordinary leaps of understanding rather than a process of rational, sequential thinking. Even when important discoveries seem like accidents, it is clear that somebody's brain was operating in such a way as to make such 'accidents' useful in their pursuit of knowledge. The 'skill' is to see the commonplace in a new light, to imagine the extraordinary and see it come to fruition. This brings some happy surprises. When a breakthrough finally comes after a long period of hard work and frustration, it comes 'out of the blue'. It seems to defy logic and leave no trace of a rational, explainable origin for all our hard thinking. This kind of brainpower happens in the very smart part of what is already the smartest living organ around. It reflects a different, more holistic level of brain processing. That's what we need to understand and exploit as personal CQ.

The scarce commodity

The scarce commodity is what we generally call creativity. It has not received proper recognition, partly because it has been associated – wrongly – with the artistic side of human endeavour, rather than with science, which has received most of the credit for the miracles of modern life. For millions of people, creativity remains veiled in mystery or ignored as trivial. Remarkably, to a large extent the mystery pervades even the highest echelons of neurophysiology and cognitive psychology. To quote (from fallible human memory) a comment by one expert: 'For all we truly understand about the human brain it might as well be stuffed with cotton wool wadding.' That was said around the turn of the last century, but the remark would sit well in a contemporary mind journal.

Weirdos and tingles

Other than the few functions, like memory or speed of response, that can be tested in a fairly scientific way, we cannot begin to understand a mental concept like creativity, let alone harness it for a purpose. It has been described as a 'self-emergent property' of our fantastically complex brain. So while space probes visit the solar neighbourhood, genetic scientists talk of the secret of life and physicists a single, cosmic equation, this unique human characteristic remains as 'serendipity', the 'Muse', the odd eureka, or the special reserve of geniuses and weirdos.

That is changing fast. The mind is again a popular topic for research. Significantly, the issues are less polarized than they used to be, between the Cartesian approach to 'mind' as separate from the brain, and the neurophysiological approach – 'top down' and 'bottom up'. Neither approach, and the narrow disciplines they spawned, has got us very far. Thankfully, psychologists and philosophers now communicate with neurologists and artificial intelligence (AI) computer technicians in a far more open and humble way. Although a long way from discovering the human mind, there is a quest for the crucial link between the mental control room and the neural engine room. Put another away, between the tingle of Beethoven or the thrill of a sunset, and the soulless, electro-chemical, synaptic firings revealed by PET scanning.

Magic

From whatever perspective, today the brain is probably the most fruitful area of scientific questioning, and remains as awesome and wonderful as ever. Put it this way; if you don't believe in magic, you need to invent your own word to describe it, and the three-pound lump that produces it. And the mysterious, creative, unconscious part of this brain accounts for the vast majority of all our thoughts and actions. It is the part that has made us what we are and will continue to create our future.

The creativity enlightenment

The modern debut of creativity dates to the inaugural address given by J P Guilford to the American Psychological Association in 1950. That was a wake-up call and stimulated lots of research and lay interest. It is now enjoying a second golden age. Conferences ranging over many disciplines now see fit to include a session on creativity. Researchers from a variety of backgrounds publish hundreds of books and articles each year on the subject. Other books, such as on management or self-development topics, may have a chapter on creativity when previously they would have just included the word in the index. More and more programmes are offered to increase our creativity, both for self-development and within a work context. Large corporations seem to have recognized the return on investment of creativity training. In particular, they try to provide an environment, or quasi-company, somewhere within the organization in which creative *people* can flourish. (Chapter 13 addresses creativity in business.) But this just underlines the very *personal* nature of creativity, and that is the approach I have taken in this book.

All things mental

The creativity enlightenment has occurred largely in the wake of a renewed interest in all things mental, the 1990s 'decade of the brain' and suchlike. It has embraced intelligence in its many forms, and equally illusive concepts such as consciousness, identity and spirituality. Like creativity, these are largely unexplored territory scientifically. Creativity offers a particularly exciting prospect, not just to study, but to personally aspire to. Like a strong currency, you can convert it into many visible products and pleasures.

The starting point of the book is simple: we are all creative by nature and potentially *very* creative. We lose much of our creativity during school years, and it is not difficult for parents, who witness the transition from home to school, to see the changes. For most adults, therefore, being more creative means no more than recovering some forgotten skills like riding a bike, swimming or playing the spoons. That need not be too hard. However long the time gap, relearning our childhood creativity is more to do with confidence and self-belief than special skills. It's a matter of stimulating and harnessing what is already there. Big C creativity becomes little c creativity in everyday life, but always with big C potential. The enlightenment in recent years has helped to answer important questions about nurture and nature and the actual workings of the creative mind.

Nature or nurture?

What about genes? If there is a genetic element, as is the received wisdom in the case of IQ-type intelligence and natural talents, few would agree that it is an overriding factor. Even the musical geniuses of history were more likely to have been raised in a domestic hothouse of musical talent than in an agricultural community with not a musical instrument within miles. In other words, their genius, insofar as it produced something of lasting value, was a product of nurture, whatever nature endowed. Scientific breakthroughs likewise usually follow years of very hard work and commitment to a specific domain, with little evidence of a genetic head start. In many cases historical creative figures were not known to be gifted children. The great railway inventor Stephenson was illiterate and almost innumerate at the age of 18 and you would not have recognized some of the biggest creative geniuses in history from their school reports.

We shall see in Chapters 8 and 9, about the environment and culture, that nothing is creative unless the people around at the time decide that it is. In other words, what we usually associate with very personal characteristics and processes has a cultural or environmental dimension that is as important – or more important – than what happens inside. Any nurture or external factor tips the creativity scales and puts more in your own hands.

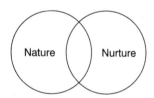

Harnessing your whole brain

It is easy to understate the potential power of creative thinking in our own lives. By confining it traditionally to artists, musicians, a handful of scientists, and geniuses generally, we fail to see its effect on ordinary lives, let alone in our own day-to-day experience. It involves nothing more or less than using your whole brain – at most, a bit of retraining and some new habits.

For most people this usually means *redressing the balance* in the underutilized creative side of the brain, and *unlearning* (of attitudes and habits) rather than learning. It is a different, but not a difficult process. However, creative thinking can bring immediate and large gains in any sphere of life.

I use the shorthand term CQ, or creativity quotient, as the degree to which we harness this unique human creative potential and put it to use in getting what we consider most important in our lives. Its effect, even when the increased quotient is a modest increment, can be dramatic in the life of an individual, and more so when released into an educational system or commercial or political organization. We cannot begin to imagine the impact of human creativity at a global level. The dramatic big C impact on technology in computers and communications in recent years is just a down payment. We can all experience creativity at a personal level and achieve something special in our lives.

2

Defining creativity

History has provided scores of definitions of creativity and none has gained popular currency. J P Guilford, one of the leading creativity experts, identified from his research no fewer than 120 characteristics of creativity in his so-called 120-factor theory. He must have applied some creativity when conceiving his prolific theory but he doesn't make it clear what creativity *is* for any practical purposes. Other researchers have come up with more moderate numbers of creativity traits, sometimes using combinations of Guilford's 120 and, to ensure confusion, changing some terminology in the process.

The question you need to ask is 'Can I get better at any of these characteristics and if so, given a single lifetime, which ones do I start on, and what do I do?' However, emulating specific characteristics may not be much better than using off-the-shelf techniques if we do not understand what creativity *means*, how its many characteristics interrelate and the sort of processes it involves. Knowledge alone is not enough. A person's motivation, for example, accounts for a large part of their creativity but doesn't figure in most definitions or psychometric tests. Nor do creativity traits allow for the environment you are operating in, whether in an organization or the wider culture to which you belong. So we need some background knowledge and basic skills. Definitions are a good place to start.

As you consider the definitions of creativity, its characteristics in individuals, processes and the products it produces, you will start to think more creatively without conscious effort, and be motivated to understand and try out more. Creative people are not just motivated in the particular task they do, but they are motivated to *being creative* as individuals. As with any subject you get deep into, your motivation will grow as you understand and practise more.

You can use your own resources of creativity which may in the past have been confined to narrow parts of your life and apply them to important, current goals. There may be some relearning to revive the creative skills you had as a child but no brain transplant is required.

Amassing definitions is not to say that we have heard the last word on what creativity is. On the contrary, our best neurophysiologists have hardly any inkling of how the brain produces creativity, or how to recognize it on a PET scan. The deeper we delve, the more complex, if not humanly incomprehensible it all seems. Psychologists are still in a quandary over the equally challenging mysteries of intelligence and consciousness, let alone creativity. A generation of behaviourists probably set us back a decade by not even considering creativity, and other 'invisible' human traits. Nevertheless, the definitions we have accumulated offer a pot pourri of creativity, from the point of view, for example, of:

▓ its component characteristics;
▓ the processes it embraces;
▓ the sort of people who are said to have exhibited it;
▓ how we might measure it;
▓ its application in science and art;
▓ its relationship to intelligence;
▓ its manifestation in biological brain processes.

The only certainty we have is that no single definition, nor even a shortlist or 'canon', has been accepted by the many fields of knowledge interested in the topic. The popular definitions, however, offer clues as to the range of perspectives we need to address in order to have an adequate working understanding of the subject and gain something of value personally. For example, here are some answers to the question 'what is creativity?':

■ something that artists possess;
■ an unusual or original approach to problems;
■ the association of disparate cognitive elements, or ideas;
■ a process that leads to a worthwhile product;
■ a self-emergent property of the brain as a complex system;
■ bringing into being something novel and useful;
■ a process that produces something original and valuable;
■ seeing the same thing as everybody else but thinking of something different;
■ the unique characteristic of what it means to be human.

Proponents of creativity have their own definitions and models, of course. A review of the different schools of thought will produce a comprehensive overview of the subject. Addressing definitions may also help to show how our ideas about creativity have evolved over time, and the key questions that any search for personal creativity raises. If you wish to be more creative, it makes sense to make your own choice of definition in any case – perhaps after reading the book.

Creative questions

Whilst there is little agreement on a definition of creativity, there is a lot of common ground on the sorts of questions we need to address to come up with one. For example:

■ Is creativity essentially about people? Or products? Or processes? These three approaches account for the main schools of thought about creativity, and form the basis – sometimes in combination – of most attempts at a definition. Each is covered in the remaining chapters of the book.

■ Is creativity a social or personal phenomenon? Put another way, should we view creativity from the point of view of the creative person, or from the point of view of the wider community who, in the end, determine whether what we create is really creative and useful? Chapters 8 and 9 address creativity and the context or environment in which it takes place.

■ Is creativity common or rare? Is it something that we all possess and use in our everyday lives, even though we don't use it to the full? Or is it a characteristic of special people, such as Einstein, Mozart or Pelé, or lesser-known people in certain 'creative' professions? Definitions span these extremes.

■ Is creativity general or 'domain-specific'? In other words, can it be applied in any discipline or a wide variety of situations, or is it related in a particular person to a specific domain, such as physics, Formula 1 racing or architecture? Do you need a different kind of creativity to compose music from the kind you need to invent a new vacuum cleaner or discover a scientific principle? The same definition dilemma applies to intelligence, with its 'multiple intelligences'.

■ Is creativity quantitative or qualitative? The wide use of psychometric instruments to measure creativity assumes that creativity can be quantified, such as how a person 'scores' on a range of creative characteristics. However, it is also seen as something quite unique to the person and only able to be valued qualitatively in that personal context. We cover psychometrics in Chapter 11.

Each of these basic questions will reappear in different forms as you consider what it means to be creative in your own life.

Attempting to answer these questions to your own satisfaction will be good start to increasing your personal creativity. As we shall see, creativity is as much to do with self-belief and motivation as with any special mental process or genetic gift. So although the world of science has not provided an acceptable definition, it helps to have your own working understanding of creativity. That way, you will know what you want, and in due course you will know whether you get it or not. That's not as difficult as it may at first seem, given the scores of conflicting definitions produced by experts. You may have already formed your own intuitive answers to the above basic questions, for instance, and you will refine them as you read on.

Popular creativity themes

A number of writers have made a particular contribution to the study of creativity. These have left us their own definitions, as well as theories, models and processes that support them. Specific *aspects* of creativity may be more helpful than any single definition, just as with intelligence and intelligence testing – especially if you want to monitor improvements. Although it is doubtful whether IQ measures true intelligence, it seems to do a good job in testing verbal and numerical skills and logical reasoning – in other words, *the things it does a good job in*. In the case of creativity we can focus on the stages, the styles (such as divergent thinking), thinking components (such as originality) or personality traits. Each is an aspect of creativity you need to understand if you want to be personally more creative, and offers plenty of scope without getting stuck on a single definition.

Convergent and divergent thinking

J P Guilford referred to the comparison between convergent and divergent thinking, and the theme recurs frequently in research and education. In brief, convergent thinking relates to the linear, logical, single-correct-answer thinking we associate with IQ tests and academia. Divergent thinking calls for multiple rather than single, black and white answers, concrete innovation rather than abstract concepts, and original or unusual ideas. It is akin to the popular concept of lateral thinking.

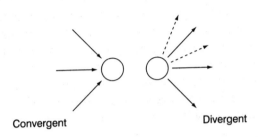

Convergent   Divergent

Guilford suggested three major creativity factors, each of which has provided a springboard for others to fill out the concepts and add their own definitions:

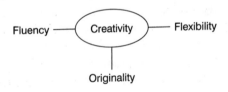

Fluency —— Creativity —— Flexibility

Originality

These thinking characteristics will have a major effect on your CQ and we shall cover them in some detail throughout the book.

Lateral and vertical thinking

Edward de Bono coined the term lateral thinking, which he compared with vertical thinking. Vertical thinking roughly equates to Guilford's convergent, linear thinking; lateral thinking equates to his non-linear, divergent thinking. When thinking vertically we tend to dig *deeper*, whereas when thinking laterally we dig *in a different place*. It is like the difference between a question with a single, correct answer and a multiple choice question – or better still, one where you can add your own, unique comments where the questionnaire says 'other'. When thinking vertically, we keep digging deeper because we know there is a 'right' answer so we must come to it eventually. In practice, we usually accept the first plausible solution that arises, assuming that is 'it'. When we are thinking laterally, *no* answer is accepted as final, however it seems to fit. There is always a better solution – or it helps our creativity to *make that assumption*. Like an Olympic record, even the very best is there to be broken. These assumptions form a sound basis for better thinking and a more fulfilling life.

Cognitive virtues

Robert J Sternberg wrote about 'cognitive virtues', and he also offered three:

Notice that he treats creativity as separate from intelligence, while others treat it as an aspect, or component, of intelligence. Sternberg considered the degree of correlation between these three factors, and found that it differed from field to field (eg business, art, physics) and that the strongest parallels were between intelligence and creativity. However, he found important differences between creativity and the other two.

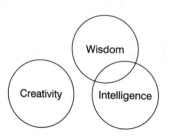

These differences were:

- ■ unconventionality in thoughts and actions;
- ■ aesthetic taste;
- ■ flexibility;
- ■ toleration of ambiguity;
- ■ questioning of authority.

These characteristics, like Guilford's 'big three' above, crop up frequently, and figure in other definitions. They are used, for instance, when deciding on which people, such as well-known artists and scientists in history, we can label as creative, to study or emulate. Practically, they point us in the direction of *how to think* and *what to do* to be creative as individuals. They also form the criteria a company must take into account in making their staff more creative.

Weisberg maintained there was no such thing as creativity. He applied his arguments to what he called the 'myths' of creativity: divergent thinking, genius and artistic creativity. The late David Bohm, perhaps one of the greatest physicists of the twentieth century, starts his book *On Creativity* with the words: 'Creativity is, in my view, something that it is impossible to define in words.'

It is strange that defining creativity didn't give other writers such a problem. Its manifold definitions have not made creativity any clearer but they have raised some of the questions we need to address personally.

If you can clearly define creativity other than in terms of what it means to you personally you may have missed the point and will at best add one more definition to the experts' motley list. It is much easier, however, and certainly more useful, to define *what creativity can do for you*, how it can help you realize your important goals and generally make life better. On such a foundation of understanding, your CQ is already on the way up.

3

Creativity and the standard brain

The circuitry of your brain, laid end to end, would reach a couple of times round the world. Your brain has enough capacity to produce extraordinary feats of creativity as well as its regular housekeeping. Although based on scanty science, it is said that even Einstein used no more than 10 per cent of his brain. Link that with the fact that the brains of highly creative and non-creative people are pretty much alike physically, and you need never doubt your potential. Boosting your CQ means using your brain in a better and different way. In this chapter you can understand the brain better and in particular its remarkable ability to produce creative thoughts that you can apply practically in your life.

Size doesn't matter

Physical size isn't what matters, nor the quality of what was inside at birth. Brains come as bulk standard and physical size makes little difference. You lose billions of your birth brain cells anyway. These are replaced by the mushrooming networks created to service your high-speed nurture in the first few years of life. Brain innards are mostly made to measure rather than off the genetic peg. As you 'think', 'imagine' and 'experience' you grow more neuronal connections into more complex networks so that within the same cranial space you can handle more thought traffic. Rather than the physical size of the lump, it's the number of synaptic connections that matter, and they are for all intents and purposes unlimited. Even old people, it has been found, grow their brains when engaged in stimulating mental activities (and incidentally, live longer).

It's a two-way process – the senses coming in, and the instructions you relay back to your body based on the meaning you create based in turn on what's already inside. As a child your physical skull grows fast anyway, but that's not because of genius genes. It provides the eventual capacity to do more or less anything you like that a brain can do, with plenty to spare. It is up to you whether you use your brain to the full.

Capacity and regional control

Although most of your brain is employed to do a variety of tasks, different regions have specialist functions. However, if you increase a region of the brain by enhancing its activity (by practice and increased complexity), you don't crowd out other regions with their own special jobs. They all grow *in number of connections* with greater use, just as a town population grows with more houses, traffic, new roads, flyovers and underpasses, yet within the original town perimeter. Your brain just gets a busier, more efficient and productive place.

It does not seem that there is any practical limit to such processes in the brain, but there are failsafe systems just in case. Most regions are multi-functional, for instance, and to a large extent one region can do the job of another – or will learn it quickly in the event of localized injury. So capacity is never a problem – but *believing that it is* can be. It can affect your confidence and self-esteem, and specifically your self-belief as to your creative ability. It works both ways: 'I'm sorry, my brain just seems to cut out', or 'I always know I will eventually come up with an answer.'

Most importantly, we are not stuck with genetic limitations. So boosting your CQ even by a large factor is a perfectly feasible choice, whatever your starting-off point. Just like a very unfit person who starts to get into shape, the less your brain has been stretched in the past the quicker you will start to realize its true potential.

Brainpower beliefs

What you believe about your brainpower is usually self-fulfilling. It will either enhance or reduce your creativity. Many people decide as children that their brains aren't up to certain things. This belief probably dates to a few chance poor marks at school and unthoughtful comments from other children or adults alike. (Children receive on average about six times as many negative comments as positive ones – sometimes hundreds in one day. That kills creativity.) In fact we are suggestible at any age, and you can create unhelpful beliefs as well as bad driving habits. As you then *act out* your unfounded belief it becomes self-fulfilling.

Fortunately, you can bring your brain up to scratch by first changing your belief in the light of better information – hence this book. You don't need to know everything – the brain defies such understanding. You need just enough information about your brain's potential to boost your self-belief as a unique, creative being. That makes everything from then on easier.

Once you accept that you have more than enough brain capacity for all manner of creativity, the transformation to real creative products will be quicker and more natural. It's only *information*, of course, much of which you have probably heard before. But by taking knowledge on board *purposefully* – with a view to using your brain more fully – it will increase your confidence in your mental resources. The most bulk-standard brain is a more or less infinite thinking machine. When the fact becomes a self-belief you will boost your own motivation to think creatively and achieve your most important goals.

Twin operating systems

Creativity is usually associated with the right side of the brain, but this is an oversimplification. The brain works holistically and the mid- and lower-brain areas are also involved. These also have right and left mirror parts, although the 'right brain' frequently refers to the neo-cortex or upper brain. The whole brain 'lights up' electrically on a scan when a person is thinking, and indeed when they are not consciously thinking, at a sort of high tickover. In any case, the left and right sides of the brain are connected by a plait of millions of fibres, so there is a lot of bicameral (two-sided) teamwork involved. It's a partnership – or is intended to be. However, just like two all-round sportspeople that excel in different individual sports, each side of your brain out-competes the other in certain kinds of mental operations, so it gets to keep the job. The two dream teams, or 'operating systems', *together* account for the unique potential creativity of your brain. For all intents and purposes it is a single system, and part of a bigger, equally integrated and interdependent mind-body system that includes emotions and every little behaviour.

Using brain-scanning techniques scientists can watch the brain at work and identify some patterns even in this twin-sided sea of seemingly chaotic activity. For example, whilst widely different parts of the brain work together for even simple functions it is possible to see where the left or right side – and indeed smaller regions – is *dominant* in neural activity. Better still, for our purposes, we can differentiate between 'creative' and 'non-creative' neural patterns. For the moment, it is significant that there are – as we would have expected – different *kinds* of thinking, or mental 'goings on'. It's one thing to instruct your foot to press a pedal in the car or put your shoes on (although you don't usually know you're doing any instructing), and another thing to think of a person's name that is on the tip of your tongue or work out how you can last out until pay day. Your brain can cope with either, but in different ways. You can trust it implicitly to do most things you do 'without thinking'.

Computer comparisons

Your brain is dynamic and you can change it simply by thinking. It is not like a solid printed circuit board, or anything solid and fixed, so computer metaphors can be misleading, in particular when considering the creative aspects of thought. For example:

■ Computer circuits are dead, while the brain is alive.

■ Computers comprise hardware that runs software whereas a brain is hardware and software (if we insist on these comparisons) *all in one*.

■ Computers crash. People do eventually but we have all sorts of reserves to pull us through normally.

■ Computers are turned off sometimes, while your brain runs round the clock for decades without major shut-downs for servicing or power cuts.

A thought does not just use existing brain circuitry, but creates new circuitry in the form of 'traces', or memories like neural fingerprints. The next sensory 'representation' you make of the outside world doesn't just tack onto the existing database, but the whole of your life experience is trawled and adjusted to make new, up-to-the-second meaning of whatever comes your way.

This fantastic, literally incomprehensible process is more like adding a new ingredient to a steaming cauldron of soup to create a slightly different flavour and consistency. On a big scale it is a two-way feedback, or cybernetic system. At any detailed level it is multi-directional in three dimensions. So the brain seems more like the chaotic interface between buyers and sellers on a stock exchange floor than a printed circuit board, except that in the brain the media are colourless waves of energy and the volume of transactions is mind-bogglingly bigger.

Self-creating organism

Your brain is continuously remaking itself. Its landscape changes just as natural topography changes with the continuous effect of rain water creating rivulets and in time great gorges. When it has done its present job it doesn't clock off, but keeps revving – like a race car ready for the starting lights – ready to respond to the next sensory bombardment. Your brain even guesses the optimal 'waiting state' to cater for what it 'thinks' will happen next (most of our lives run on habits) and thus save a few milliseconds. That tiny edge gives us a unique survival advantage. In some cases we act before we know what we are acting for. Even while you are right now thinking about that ... your brain is doing its 're-file' (like a librarian does every evening), and 'meaning' (association) tasks. It can thus let you know what you think about what you are reading in such a vivid, seamless way that you feel as if you're living out the story. Put plainly, unlike a computer, the human brain *thinks for itself*. It is a self-creating organism that shapes its environment and is at the same time shaped by it. It is not just your interpreter of the world, it *creates* your world.

This soup-like combination of electrical impulses and chemical reactions produces a configuration, or structure, that is dynamic and evolving. This has special importance for creativity. Most of what we do is routine, or soon becomes so. That is part of the neural wizardry. It means the brain can *anticipate* when and in what sequence you need to carry out actions – a mental syntax. That spells *efficiency*. It demands minimum neural activity based on the tiniest of clues – such as when you *intend* to reach out a hand to drink a cup of coffee. A simple wish sets the whole cosmos of your brain into action. It is well on with the job before you move the first muscle. If you change your mind, it is already marshalling resources for your new intention while you are still reaching for the coffee. This allows a seamless progression from standby, expected or *imagined* mode to the real thing. Just as a movie is formed from lots of still pictures, our continuous flow of consciousness comprises the half-second bits of words and actions we can consciously cope with plus the millions of sensory bits we can't. It is called being alive and conscious of it.

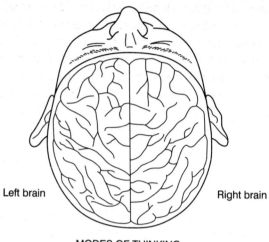

MODES OF THINKING

Left brain	Right brain
Deals with verbal ideas and uses words to describe things	Aware of things but does not connect them with words – uses gestures or pictures in description
Analysis: breaks things down into their constituent parts	Synthesizes: puts parts together to form a whole
Uses symbols to represent things	Sees things as they are
Abstracts relevant pieces of information from the whole	Makes analogies and sees likenesses
Good sense of time	Poor sense of time
Relies on facts and reasoning	Relies on intuition and instinct
Good sense of numbers	Poor sense of numbers
Poor sense of spatial relationships	Good sense of spatial relationships
Logical	Intuitive
Thinks linearly – one idea follows another	Thinks holistically – sees patterns linking ideas as a whole

However, whenever signals arise that are novel and unexpected, the 'up and running' neural patterns close down so that you can give your full attention to identifying, classifying and responding to the new situation. A sort of hush takes place, during which time the brain gets coiled up tight, ready for lightning action or to revert to a standby, 'busy' mode in the event of a false alarm. In fact, your whole body may stop, such as when you hear an unexpected knock or strange cry and freeze for a moment. You get *chemically prepared* – a heady cocktail of adrenalin for your body and noradrenalin for your brain. Additionally, or in order to be prepared to act, your brain does a high-speed recognition job. Once the signals are happily identified and classified (it's not a *real* grizzly), it returns to its restless, shifty standby mode. It has transformed itself into a new brain ready for the rest of life.

Your brain will cope smoothly with 99 per cent of what it receives as most of our lives are relegated to habits. Your brain has long since learnt to cater economically for hundreds of routine activities as well as surprises, with its sci-fi early warning and retrieval systems. That means it can divert all its power into the clever, creative work whenever you call upon it.

The bicameral partnership

Nobel prize-winner Roger Sperry did important research in the 1960s from which we understand the very different ways in which the two sides of the brain operate. Sperry's patients had the sides of their brain separated by cutting the joining bundle of fibres known as the corpus callosum. Ignoring the clinical aspects of his work (which were successful), some of the patients acted afterwards as though they were two personalities in one, sometimes showing conflict between one side and the other. For instance, a patient might physically fight, hand to hand, over the choice of which blouse to wear. Having isolated the two sides of the brain for the first time in human subjects, Sperry went on to conduct experiments that confirmed the respective functions of each hemisphere. The characteristics of

the right side closely relate to what we have come to understand as 'creative' thinking. The fundamental difference in the
way each side works helps to explain the difference between
convergent, logical, IQ-type intelligence and divergent or
lateral thinking.

Remembering that this was in the 1960s, before we had reliable scanning techniques, his findings were remarkable and
impacted neurophysiology and psychology for years ahead. My
first book, entitled *The Right Brain Manager*, reflected the trend
in thinking. The following are the characteristics commonly
related to each side of the upper brain, or neo-cortex:

■ Left hemisphere
  - Verbal: words to name, define, and describe
  - Analytic: step by step
  - Logical: rational approach
  - Sequential and linear: arranges in consecutive succession
  - Systematic and formal: methodical processing and problem solving
  - Symbolic: use of words and numbers to mean something more
  - Factual: deals with details or features of a thing
  - Abstract: theoretical, intellectual, idealistic
  - Digital: uses numbers as in counting
  - Methodical: organizes, classifies, categorizes
  - Practical: concerned with cause and effect, purpose and use
  - Rational: reason and factual data
  - Motor: controls right-side sensory organs and bodily movements

    – Learns through phonetic, analytic methods
    – Evaluates performance according to a standard
    – Outlines rather than summarizes

■ Right hemisphere

– Nonverbal:	responds to music, body language, touch
– Synthetic:	arranging parts to form a whole
– Intuitive:	follows hunches and feelings
– Causal and informal:	deals with information on basis of need or interest
– Concrete:	relates to things sensorily rather than abstractly
– Holistic:	sees whole things all at once, overall patterns
– Visual:	uses imagery, responds to pictures, colours and shapes
– Sensory:	oriented toward physical
– Spatial:	relates parts to the whole
– Responsive:	listens to music with emotion
– Originative:	interest in ideas and theories
– Motor:	controls left-side sensory organs and bodily movement

    – Learns through 'sight' or 'by ear'
    – Sensitive to fantasy, poetry, metaphor and myths
    – Timeless, continuous and free

The left side of the brain has long been associated with language and other symbolism such as mathematics, logic and step-by-step reasoning. Patients with damage to the left side, for instance, often have speech difficulties. Similarly, patients with right-side damage, such as following a stroke, often have difficulty with spatial awareness, such as finding their way from room to room.

For a while these hemispherical descriptions of the brain were associated with different activities such as music and art (right) and maths and language (left). However, we have more recently come to understand that the brain works far more holistically than first thought. 'Hemispherical specialization' concerns not so much what the brain does but *the way it does it*. The concentrated firing patterns revealed by EEGs and PET scans of the left side reveal the basic language processing and other simple distinctions in the above list. But the more dispersed right-side activity also reveals different dimensions of language processing happening concurrently – in fact, what we would loosely call the creative part of language.

Humour and innuendo

For example, the straightforward symbolic aspects of language and repetitive application of rules and logical manipulation of numbers seem to do well in the left brain. Here, networks of cells packed close together fire in harmony, reflecting the specific idea or detail being represented – like 'chair', or 'the chair broke'. However, when it comes to poetry, humour and the creative and intuitive aspects of language, the holistic right-brain specialization seems to be called upon. In this right side neural firings are more widely spread, as though an overall representation is being made – the whole *meaning* of, say, a pun or line of poetry rather than the meaning of just the words and grammar at face value. 'The chair broke' may take us back to a chair breaking a dozen years ago, or a film we saw, or any personal association with 'chair', or a connection we make between the speaker and chair. That needs holistic, right-brain searching to produce whole-brain meaning in a 'gestalt moment'. In reading or listening to prose of any sort, and especially creative or humorous material, *both* kinds of processing are required to make sense of it.

Roughly speaking, the right brain is doing the reading between the lines, the big-picture association job – what we think of as the creative part. The left brain is handling the basis syntax and 'dictionary meanings'. The basic differentiation applies to all the functions such as maths and logic that we previously pigeon-holed to the left brain. However, other more creative functions that we label as right-brain also have their equivalent detail, or close-up dimension. These depend just as much on the left brain for their close-up, 'tree' rather than 'forest' view operations.

Music and poetry to your brain

Take music. We usually think of music as creative and strongly affecting emotions, and typically in the right-brain province. However, some aspects of music require thinking patterns no less logical and rigorous than straightforward maths and language. Listeners to music, as well as composers and instrumentalists, can get pleasure in understanding the structure and symmetry of musical composition as well as enjoying the emotional tingle. This applies when we focus on any aspect of the detail or structure of a piece. The more we know about music the more we will tend to be analytical and use left-brain as well as right-brain functions. This whole-brain processing reflects these holistic (right-side) and detailed, or literal (left-side) aspects. So music is a whole-brain phenomenon, represented through these lateralized processes.

The same applies to literature. Left-brains skills are needed when poring over line-by-line detail in, say, a legal document or instruction manual. But when reading a novel, or humorous non-fiction, you call upon the right brain which pulls together *meaning* from all your past experience. Emotions are also associated with this side, and these elusive functions extend to the lower, primeval parts of the brain as well as the neo-cortex. Radical surgery to the right brain can leave a person without humour and emotions – zombie-like even though otherwise literate and intelligent. Thus it is this extra dimension to thinking that makes us uniquely human and 'alive'.

As we saw, it works both ways. What are apparently left-brain activities call upon right-brain functions. Mathematicians often see beauty and symmetry in formulae that seem to call upon an almost artistic sense, and certainly a free imagination. Not surprisingly, therefore, some of the greatest mathematicians and artists are known to have excelled in the way they used both sides of their brain and especially their imagination. Einstein the scientist indulged in extra-terrestrial leaps of imagination and childlike curiosity, going for cosmic rides on beams of light. Conversely, Beethoven the musician paid scrupulous attention to detail and structure in composition.

Similarly the classical artists were known for their sense of balance, proportion, perspective and form as well as right-brain originality and raw artistry. In each case it was the *combined* dimensions of thinking that created the genius. Although an oversimplification, the left–right brain distinction is a useful analogy for such a fundamental aspect of creative thinking.

Reconciling opposites

In every case it is the reconciliation of what seem to be *opposites*, or diametrically different perspectives, that creates unique meaning, whatever the *content* of the thinking. Which kind of operation *dominates* at any time will depend on the stage in the creative process and the demands of the task you happen to be doing. It also depends on where your holistic, intuitive side cares to take you in its mental wanderings. The right side is closely related to unconscious thought processes (the background whole-brain 'trawl' and 'incubation'), so you don't have much control over this side. On the other hand, *conscious* attention is associated with what happens on the left side and what we usually think of as proper 'thinking'. You can do something about both: 1) conscious thinking by *consciously thinking*, through a simple exercise of the will; 2) unconscious thinking by adopting *states of mind* conducive to 'subterranean', creative thinking, and a lifestyle that supports it.

Most creativity techniques require left-brain skills, even if designed to do the contrary. The more right-brain 'divergent thinking' techniques depend on a relaxed, 'not trying' state, and many other factors we met on the creativity definitions. These are not teachable in an orthodox sense but are there for you to rediscover and improve with simple practice.

Dual brain training

To be creative you need to use your whole brain. That requires health and fitness like any other part of the body. Health means a good blood supply and freedom from the many toxins that limit intellectual functioning. Fitness comes through practice and repetition – just as when training physically. In the case of creativity training it means stretching yourself with ever-new challenges to get the best out of your mind, just as a top athlete does to remain in peak form physically.

The different processes in the left and right sides of the brain require different sorts of stimuli and training. Most of the memory and academic work we are familiar with is good training for the left brain. In most cases, due to the influence of our left-brain-biased education and institutions, we are 'left-brain dominant'. So, relatively speaking at least, that side of the brain will tend to be in better shape. Doing puzzles and IQ tests – which are mostly 'conscious' thinking tasks with a single right answer – is fine. Left-brain 'catch up' training may apply to people who have a great imagination but don't seem to get down to produce anything worth while and have difficulty explaining themselves ('she seems to be in another world'). That's the exception rather than the rule, however, and in this book we are concerned with boosting creativity and what are loosely termed right-brain skills. In any case you can do both kinds of training in parallel. Real-life problems require both right and left brain skills *together*.

You can easily check whether you are left- or right-brain dominant from the quick exercise on pages 39 and 40. A longer brain dominance test is included in my book *The Right Brain Manager*. These exercises may confirm what you already knew about yourself. However, they illustrate that these personality differences reflect *normal* thinking processes that happen to be used in a habitually biased way. Closely matched right and left brain 'scores' are not significant. If you are heavily left-brain dominant you should benefit a lot from the book, although some ideas may seem strange. You may want to do the same questionnaire after getting to know the subject and carrying out the booster programme at the end.

The right brain doesn't operate according to either formulae or neat schedules, and will not respond to a deadline. Nor will creative thinking always have a 'right' answer, so conventional memory skill and rote learning doesn't do much for your CQ. Most creative people cannot be tied down in that way anyway. Sadly, most people do not stay creative into adulthood as the school system educates imagination out of them. In this case 'practice' and 'know how' are more to do with the ability to relax and 'turn off' than with intellectual powers of focus and memory. These skills are covered as part of creativity conditioning in Chapter 14. As we have seen, the right side of the brain takes a wider, peripheral view, but at the same time *integrates* the lower-level symbolic representation in which the left brain specializes. That way you see both the trees and the forest, 'read between the lines', get the hidden meaning and appreciate the subtlest of humour. Although we are sometimes 'in two minds', it is amazing how two such different brains continuously act as one and display their synergy in surprising creativity.

Understanding your brain

Sadly, millions of people go to their graves without recapturing their childhood sense of wonder and curiosity and freedom to question. As adults we may need strong resolution and a figurative bash on the head to dislodge the entrenched brain patterns we have accumulated. From there on it is easy, exciting sailing. You just need to stay mentally healthy with routine services. It starts with understanding what your brain can do, how to turn it on, what to do and what not to do to think at your best.

Trying too hard

We all know of times when the harder you try to remember something the more difficult it becomes. Likewise, the more conscious mental effort you apply to a problem the more you seem to be hitting a brick wall. The answer in such cases comes out of the blue, when you are thinking of something else – not apparently related – or nothing much at all. In other words, when in a more 'freewheeling' state. Sometimes a good night's sleep does the trick.

This receptive yet inattentive state involves *attitude* more than intellectual skill, and is certainly not a function of IQ as we measure it. Nor does uninhibited thinking come naturally to most people over about six years of age. A hands-on, focused, down-to-earth executive may find great difficulty in relaxing, even for a short period. He or she thus squeezes out whatever creativity might have been there and misses out on innovative ideas that can save time, solve problems and make money. A

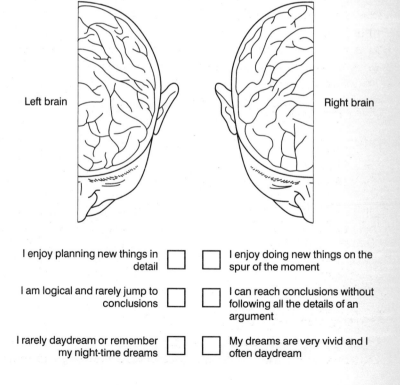

Left brain   Right brain

I enjoy planning new things in detail ☐	☐ I enjoy doing new things on the spur of the moment
I am logical and rarely jump to conclusions ☐	☐ I can reach conclusions without following all the details of an argument
I rarely daydream or remember my night-time dreams ☐	☐ My dreams are very vivid and I often daydream

Left brain			**Right brain**
I try to find the reasons behind other people's behaviour	☐	☐	I can rarely see the motivation behind other people's behaviour
I prefer mathematical and scientific subjects to artistic subjects	☐	☐	I prefer artistic subjects to mathematical and scientific subjects
I am punctual and have a good sense of time	☐	☐	I am rarely punctual and have a poor sense of time
I am good at describing my feelings in words	☐	☐	I find it difficult to put my feelings into words
I rely on the evidence when making a decision	☐	☐	I rely on my feelings when making a decision
My files and reference materials are in perfect order	☐	☐	I rarely bother to file things
I keep my hands still when I am talking	☐	☐	I gesture a lot when I am talking
I rarely have hunches and prefer not to follow my intuition	☐	☐	I rely on my instincts and follow my hunches
I rarely think in visual terms	☐	☐	My impression and thoughts often appear in pictures
I am good at explaining things	☐	☐	I can understand what someone means without being able to explain it
I solve problems by keeping at them and trying different approaches until I find a solution	☐	☐	I solve problems by putting them to the back of my mind and waiting for a solution to come up
I am very good at puzzles and word games	☐	☐	I do not enjoy puzzles and word games
I have my feelings well under control	☐	☐	I let my feelings show
I prefer reading non-fiction to romantic novels	☐	☐	I prefer reading romantic novels to non-fiction
I analyse problems	☐	☐	I deal with a problem as a whole
I am not particularly musical	☐	☐	I am very fond of music
Score	☐	☐	

conventional, 'do it now' management training course will probably *reinforce* such a style and perpetuate the problem. A few days' break doing something relaxing and enjoyable but completely out of character may be enough to bring a person to their creative senses.

When it comes to creative thinking the brain seems to have a mind of its own. It has its own special way of processing thoughts, including what we think of as creative thoughts, and needs to be left to get on with it in most cases. We don't know much about the way it does this, and most of our language is metaphorical and analogical. But we do know that you cannot buck the system and expect your brain to do what it is not inclined to do. Fortunately, without knowing the intricate workings of the brain, you can induce a more creative state simply by relaxing and not trying too hard. There are plenty of effective ways to relax and most people have their favourite method. With further practice and feedback you can become more in tune with your inner self and start to control both the way you think and the content of your thought. That is the essence of intrapersonal intelligence and self-awareness, aspects of emotional intelligence or EQ. You can use what you have learnt about the brain in metaphors and analogies to help you to be *practically* more creative.

Emotion and creativity

The creative operations of the brain are also closely linked with emotions. You can't separate emotion from thinking, just as you can't separate the body from the mind. Like self-beliefs, emotions can be positive or negative, and either enhance or inhibit your creativity. Creative events and periods are usually associated with pleasure and even a feeling of elation, and that is no coincidence. It is a feature of creative 'highs', during which 'happy' chemicals are pumped round your brain. Control over this part of your mind means control over the emotions that accompany creative thinking. Like most functions in the mind–body system, we create feedback systems that produce either a virtuous or vicious cycle of feelings and behaviour. Belief in your own creativity creates positive results in your life and increases your self-esteem, which in turn affects your emotion – you *feel* better. You then proceed to more challenging creative tasks and a self-fulfilling cybernetic process has begun. Emotion helps to explain the extraordinary degree of self-motivation creative people summon up.

Self resources

Most people have a positive self-belief in some area of their life in which they get pleasure and exercise creativity as a matter of course. It is usually a sport, hobby or special interest they happen to be good at and enjoy. This is a valuable resource. You can recall past occasions when you were specially creative and 'anchor' them so that you can recall the state whenever you feel the need (covered in Chapter 14). It makes sense to use your own resources first. With a bit of practice you will vividly re-experience a past creative state and 'turn it on' easily. The anchor and the kinaesthetic state it triggers are permanently linked – it becomes another brain pattern, or habit. New successes provide new inner resources and hence the virtuous cycle of creativity.

Once in the right state, creative thinking and behaviour come naturally. The real power of such existing 'state' resources is in applying them to areas of your life in which you are less confident. These can be critical parts of your life such as work and social situations, so any change has a lot of leverage and boosts both your self-belief as a creative person and your confidence generally. Relaxation and different forms of meditation do a similar job, and you need to relax anyway when carrying out memory recall exercises like this. Rather than techniques and formulae, understanding and using your brain better is the way to increasing your CQ and producing tangible results.

Accessing alpha

Some experimental research we cover later in Chapter 12 has linked creativity to the ability to enter an 'alpha' brainwave state. In this state your body is relaxed and your brain 'unbusy', yet you are able to focus clearly as if in a hypnotic state. You are *aware of being aware*. This state has been widely associated with creativity, and the state of mind during which creative times happen. The period before falling off to sleep is a very receptive time creatively, for instance.

Alpha is a natural state, but that doesn't mean that we adopt it as 'naturally' as we do other, faster brain states such as 'hard', external focus. This varies from person to person as our personalities do, but it is amenable to change. Thinking styles are habits. Like behavioural habits, it just takes application and practice to change them. In particular, you can adopt the alpha state more purposely rather than in the odd daydreaming session. It can apply both to general creativity training or conditioning and also when faced with specific challenging situations that demand a creative mind.

You can improve this ability to control your brain by relaxation training and regular practice. The secret is to get into the *habit* of relaxing at different periods, however short, during the day and every day. If this is not familiar to you personally, you probably know people who seem to be able to turn off and 'go inside' their own world. It should be a way of life, and affect your attitude, rather than be something you have to will yourself to do – although at first you will have to do it consciously. Going 'vacant-eyed' may seem a cop-out at the time, and might be misunderstood in a busy work environment. Daydreaming has negative connotations, as children realize when they move from kindergarten to school. However, this is the way to harness your unconscious mind and get your creative brain operating in the way it likes to. In fact, relaxation and control over brain frequency have advantages far beyond creativity, and can positively affect your health, temperament and general well-being.

4

Creative people

What sort of a personality is a creative person likely to have? What personal traits do they exhibit? Over the years researchers have tried to identify the characteristics of creative individuals. All of us are creative, of course, in the sense that our creativity is what makes us uniquely human. In a very real sense, for example, what we think about most, we tend to create in our lives, or *become*. That is a higher-order creativity than making widgets or building cathedrals. Yet a cursory historical review shows that the great advances in art and science can be credited to a tiny minority rather than the mass of creative humanity.

Is the human creativity that has given us civilization to be credited to a handful of geniuses or should we all get the credit? Likewise, can we learn from the lives of these few geniuses or the person in the next office, or should we learn more about how to use the creative resources we all possess?

Creative thinking traits

Plastic personality

Personal differences may concern the *personality* of the person – the sort of life-long traits we put down more to luck or genetics than choice. This applies also to so-called 'natural' gifts, such as musical or artistic talent that appears at an early age. Such personality traits as risk taking and independence, for example, have been linked with creative people. In fact, the potential effect of our environment, life circumstances and early education will probably account for the lion's share of the personality we find we have as adults. As we saw in the previous chapter, a new baby's brain is packed with far more cells than it will ever use, and most become redundant as its environment dictates the patterns it needs and, in effect, creates its made-to-measure personality. Before long we start to select our own environment and as an adult make deliberate brain changes by reflection, imagining, thinking and deciding. Similarly, we mould our 'plastic' personality by the lifestyle we adopt and consciously practise whatever behaviour and thought patterns we want to perfect. That all tips the balance in favour of nurture over nature. It is mostly self-nurture, or the power of thinking. So a person has to be rather careless or uninformed to allow unwanted parents' personality traits to repeat themselves.

The continuously changing structure of the brain is, in effect, a high-speed evolutionary process unique to highly developed conscious thought – as near as you get to self-programming. So, whatever your genetic heritage, you can *outweigh* it by conscious, purposeful natural selection a million times faster than hitherto. There are now techniques, drawn mainly from neuro-linguistic programming, to change fundamental behaviours even at a high personality level, previously thought to be fixed for life.

Attitude and emotion

Attitude will also affect a person's creativity. You will probably approach one task very differently to another, or change in your 'intrinsic motivation' from day to day and for no known reason. This pendulum, more emotive sort of thinking is more easily changeable than a long-term personality trait, of course.

Meeting a cheerful person in the morning, or receiving a welcome letter or telephone call, can change your whole attitude for hours. Creativity experiments have shown that this is one of the variables we can learn to control. It affects a person's underlying way of thinking rather than observable behaviour, and can thus instantly affect a whole range of behaviours. More than anything, attitude reflects a person's motivation, whether intrinsic (pleasure in the task for its own sake) or extrinsic (in response to external recognition or reward). Chapters 9 to 11 show the effectiveness of different interventions on motivation and creativity. Usually, buying a book on a particular subject confirms your positive attitude and initial motive. Thereafter, motivation can quickly grow naturally as you take interest in new knowledge and experiences. On the 80/20 rule, self-motivation is one of the factors that can make a big difference with a little effort.

Innate creativity

We witness creativity in the most mundane of circumstances and in ordinary people everywhere. It is a condition of human functioning. For instance, creativity draws on past sensory experience and we can all generate more than our discrete 'store' of experiences. You do that whenever you chat to somebody, read a magazine article or travel abroad. By putting two or more bits of understanding together your creative brain can produce an extraordinary new insight. Young children, for example, to whom almost everything is a new experience, often come out with profoundly creative insights ('Out of the mouths of babes and sucklings'). Most important perhaps, we all use the same basic mental processes that the geniuses – and children – use. As we saw in the previous chapter, this is not a matter of brain size, but innate creativity.

The two conditions for creativity usually cited are originality and usefulness, or utility. The 'everyday', innate creativity I refer to largely fits this definition. How many times have you had the spark of an idea that solved a problem at a stroke or made a task much easier? It would be unfair to make 'a contribution to the advance of civilization' a criterion for creativity. Most of us are interested in our own lives and ambitions and would prefer to be recognized for our creativity while we are around to appreciate it. Having said that, given average intelligence, our creative potential is more or less unlimited so we don't have to stick to the small-time.

Doers and dreamers

Some people act on their ideas, while others don't. The latter are more likely to be classed as 'dreamers' living in their own inner world, so they don't fulfil the 'usefulness' criterion. That doesn't mean ideas on their own are of no value. In the case of creative artists, the creativity itself, or the idea, may be the 'product'. In some controversial modern art, execution, or artistic skill, plays a minimal part. In creative or extempore dance, the creativity is in the dance. Neither dancer nor spectators take away a tangible product, but the value gained in the creative act itself may outmatch a more utilitarian outcome.

In any event creativity depends on an audience or some context and can only be defined within a culture that happens to recognize such creativity. Thus usually the creative 'product' – such as a tangible consumer product or service – determines the creativity of the person who produced it. As with modern art, the buyers or beneficiaries collectively will determine whether a product has creative, or any kind of value.

We can discount the da Vincis and Einsteins of history and even the lottery of genetics: when it comes to human creativity the playing field is as level as it gets. As a personality trait, creativity is as universal as they come. We have a lot going for us in the spirit of curiosity and love for life that we are blessed with as children. But we have a lot going against us in our 'left-brain' education and institutions, so innate creativity just bubbles to the surface in limited parts of our lives. In fact it can bubble anywhere. The aim is for more bubbles, but also the skill to identify and use them.

Genius and giftedness

Creative people differ greatly, not just in the creative products they produce, but also in the recognition they get. Put another way, we differ in the extent to which society, and our chosen domain of interest, values our product. Otherwise, it is a matter of degree. Some people are considered *particularly* creative and this is the sort of 'creative person' that we are concerned with most. We can learn from the way they think and emulate the way they behave.

The psychology of genius

The idea of genius, as well as 'giftedness' in children, or prodigies, has fascinated people for centuries. Extreme examples have the advantage that they are universally credited with creative excellence so we don't argue over whether they were creative or not. More anonymous contemporary examples such as in modern art or popular music, or the creative person down the street, might not be considered appropriate models. At the same time, noteworthy examples give us a condensed, stark view of the creative person, which makes it easier to understand the creative process and identify the sort of creative products such people produce. In this light, creativity is not abstract but personified. By considering the best examples we can find, we are likely to find something worth emulating. Rather than just admiring traits we wish we had, it is more useful to learn what these people did with the same brain resources you and I have.

Francis Galton was not the first to study genius, but he has become known as the father of historiometry which is the study of behaviour based on eminent historic individuals. The term came from Frederick Woods in a 1909 paper entitled *A New Name for a New Science* – the new name being historiometrics. By studying lives, usually of eminent people about whom we have enough biographical data, over the long term, it looks for laws and relationships that would not be apparent when looking at specific events, dates and places. Woods defined it in this way: 'The facts of history of a more personal nature have been subjected to statistical analysis by some more or less objective method.' He thought that the new science would be particularly useful for the study of the psychology of genius.

The emphasis in historiometry is on measurement, so the rich homilies of history have to be converted, for example, into IQ (retroactively, as IQ is a more recent concept). Analysis of the data then reveals the otherwise hidden relationships and factors at work. In the case of creativity, the search is with historical individuals (usually long since dead) who are generally known to have exhibited creative genius. The odd living Nobel prize winner might also be included, but in each case the individual will have made a significant contribution to a particular domain of human achievement. Historiometric studies do not only focus on single persons, but cover multiple cases – even thousands – so that significant conclusions can be drawn when the information is analysed.

The most important example of this approach to creativity is in the monumental work of Catharine Cox. It started with Lewis M Terman, who adapted the original Binet–Simon intelligence test into English, producing what eventually became known as the Stanford–Binet test. To validate the consequences of having a high IQ, Terman initiated a famous longitudinal study of children he identified as intellectually gifted. This resulted in a series of books collectively entitled *Genetic Studies of Genius*. Inspired by Frederick Woods, he thought it might be feasible to estimate IQ scores for eminent individuals based on biographical data and published a seminal paper entitled *The Intelligence Quotient of Francis Galton in Childhood*. Then Catharine Cox, a graduate student of Terman, decided to take the same technique that Terman applied to Galton to obtain comparable IQ scores for about 300 eminent individuals, 200 of whom were world famous for their creativity. She turned Terman's study round the other way, and hoped to show that those who receive distinction as adults would have been selected as intellectually gifted children if they had been given the

Stanford–Binet test. This work became the second volume of the *Genetic Studies of Genius* series.

Traits of eminence

Cox went further. She set aside a group of 100 eminent subjects for a special analysis in which she could assess their measure of achieved eminence on 67 (10 up on Heinz) character traits. Many researchers continued to use this biographical approach, such that historiometry has become an important contribution to our understanding of creativity, especially from the point of view of the creative person.

Studies of outstanding creative individuals reveal some important factors that we would be unlikely to notice if we just considered creativity as something we all have and use, although to a far lesser degree. For example:

- ■ Highly creative people are usually associated with one main domain, or discipline, and they seem to give their lives over to this.
- ■ The work is usually complex, prolonged and demanding, whatever the sphere.
- ■ Creative 'products', such as notable works of art or scientific discoveries, or recognition do not come quickly.
- ■ Their single-mindedness tends to affect family and other relationships.
- ■ Creativity at this lofty level involves conflicts and personal sacrifices.

These keep recurring. For example, it takes perhaps 10 years of specialized training to become competent in a domain, be it physics, ballet or fiction writing. Then further years to produce a creative work that is recognized as such by the field, or judges within that domain.

Many famous creators did not sustain long-term relationships, and even those that had wives and families, such as Einstein, Freud, Gandhi and Picasso, had relationship problems. Einstein recalled: 'I lived in solitude in the country and noticed how the monotony of quiet life stimulates the creative mind.'

Even the more extrovert high creators such as Picasso did not get deeply involved with any one person in their extensive social interactions. As part of a sort of bargain to maintain their life work, most sacrificed non-work-related activities, as well as relationships. Some would work for days and weeks focused on a single issue, in their own world of thought. In the extreme they became slaves to their goals and the challenges they faced.

Gardner's exemplary creators

Research into highly creative individuals has confirmed these traits and added further intriguing factors, such as those Howard Gardner identifies in his *Exemplary Creators*:

- birth in an area at some distance from a centre of culture;
- a regular bourgeois childhood, with a strict disciplinary regime at home;
- discovering other young people with similar talents and ambition;
- selection of a domain from a limited range of options;
- willingness to challenge authority, either directly or through the creation of unorthodox creative works;
- up to a decade mastering a domain before their first major, recognized work;
- a slow realization that current thinking in the domain is fundamentally flawed;
- exploration of areas that are considered dangerous or remote;
- a feeling of isolation;
- the importance of support at the time of a breakthrough.

Some of these seem innocuous until they are seen to repeat themselves over the generations and in very different spheres.

Patterns have also been identified after the main creative break-through (for which the person is best known) and in later life. For instance, subsequent breakthroughs tend to happen also at approximate 10-year intervals. Later breakthroughs tend to be more integrative and less abrupt than earlier ones. But plenty of 'normal' characteristics are apparent in later life. For example, these individuals sometimes identify uses of their work alien to their own intent, and they have to make the decision whether to oppose or ignore this – they are not immune to outside opinion, pressures and plagiarism. Not caring much for others, they are often at great risk of personal trauma. As geniuses get older they become more and more identified with their work, as the only thing that counts.

Many highly creative individuals lost one or both parents when young. And there are correlations between certain disorders, like manic depressive disease, and certain creative behaviours such as writing fiction – but we don't know which is cause and which is effect. Having said that, we also know that most orphans and mentally disturbed people do not stand out as especially creative. If anything, historiometric studies show that geniuses are very human indeed and seem to stand out as much for their single-mindedness and motivation as for their unusual mental gifts.

Creating opportunities

Creative people often stand out from the rest of society as a little 'different' and this creates its own kind of problems. However, what seems to be significant is the way they deal with setbacks and disappointments, whether in their work or with people. Rather than change their job or become despond-ent, they tend to exploit differences and conflict by converting them into advantages. Freud, for instance, from an impover-ished Jewish family, wanted to pursue a career in science. When he failed to achieve status as a world-class researcher, he exploited his particular strengths in the linguistic and interpersonal areas to create a new quasi-scientific domain called psychoanalysis. Einstein, an indifferent student (so he said), stood out in the way he combined his mathematical and spatial gifts. This ability to turn situations around and see new perspectives seems as much a personality trait as a special creativity characteristic, yet it is clearly a major factor in creative accomplishment.

These many features of creative people don't condense easily into a short list of exemplary characteristics. But there are some factors which are common to both historic creative figures and recognized contemporary achievers in science and the arts. Highly creative people are certainly in the positive rather than negative thinking camp. They tend to see problems and setbacks as challenges and opportunities. During the past century at least, creative people as a category have not had it any easier than others. Their achievement stems from their personalities, beliefs and attitude to life, plus a better use of the standard brain they were equipped with. Here are more personal factors that support the positive, opportunity-seeking perspective of creative people:

- They tend to reflect a great deal on their goals, their success in achieving them, and the lessons they learn from the times when they don't achieve what they set out for.
- They recognize and analyse their own strengths and weaknesses, and apply their strengths to the optimum.
- They do not bemoan areas of their lives in which they are less gifted or wallow in self-pity.
- They tend to reframe defeats and failures as opportunities for greater achievement and learning.

Whilst these personality features are usually included in lists of characteristics in some form or other, these lists do not indicate their weighted importance in the life of the creative person. They reflect general ways of thinking and attitude rather than special processes of divergent thinking. Any one of these key factors, linked to time and place circumstances, could account for a person's creative productivity. The French economist Jean Monnet said what many other creative people over the centuries have said in so many words: 'I regard every defeat as an opportunity.' Motivation – in its many forms and from whatever causes – seems to play a greater part than intelligence or even some special creative gift.

Characteristics of creative thinking

The characteristics of creative people have not just emerged from the study of genius. We can now draw upon more recent, extensive work in cognitive psychology and especially though the widespread use of psychometric instruments. From this, characteristics have been identified which are too numerous to be taken account of in experiments. Moreover, they reflect creativity in the ordinary person rather than from the examples of creative geniuses we have met. They are far too varied for one person to aspire to, although one or two key characteristics can make a big difference to a person's creative output. They do, however, make a good start at identifying what CQ comprises, and you will find yourself measuring your own tendencies against them. In particular, more recent studies have focused more on particular thinking characteristics rather than the personality of the person. This gets closer to the *process* of creative thinking that we cover in Chapter 5.

So-called 'ideational fluency' is the thinking trait that seems to embody the various characteristics usually cited. Many in the following section are based on an article by J P Guilford in 1959, and most of the others in the list mirror these in substance. Indeed, surprisingly little has changed over decades in the range of common 'creativity characteristics'. Thankfully, the list is not as long as a typical list applying to the *intelligent* person or the 'traits of a good leader'.

Guilford's article reports on a study in which subjects took tests measuring various aptitudes or skills, and were also rated for creativity. If the score for an aptitude or skill correlates well with creativity ratings, then that aptitude or skill is held to be an important characteristic of creative people. The descriptions of common characteristics that follow are brief but you will meet some of these later:

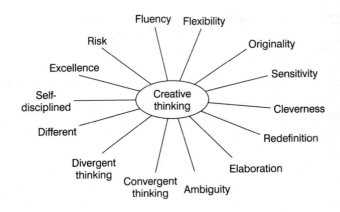

■ **Fluency of thinking**. The person is able to think freely and effortlessly. It comprises:
  - word fluency – can easily state words containing a given letter or combination of letters;
  - associational fluency – can easily state synonyms for a given word;
  - expressional fluency – can easily write well-formed sentences with a specified content;
  - ideational fluency – can easily produce ideas to fulfil certain requirements (for example, to name objects that are hard, white and edible) or to write an appropriate title for a given story.
■ **Flexibility of thinking**. The person can easily abandon old ways of thinking and adopt new ones. For example:
  - Spontaneous flexibility – can produce a great variety of ideas such as the popular 'uses for a common

object'. For example, in suggesting uses for a brick, the person can jump among categories, from building material to door stop to missile to source of red powder.

- Adaptive flexibility – can generalize requirements of a problem to find a solution. For example, in a problem of forming squares using a minimum number of lines, can abandon the usual idea that all squares have to be the same size.

■ **Originality**. The person comes up with ideas that are statistically unusual. An example is remote associations: the person forms associations between elements that are remote from each other in time or space or remote from each other logically.

■ **Ability to see or sensitivity to problems**. The person can state difficulties or deficiencies in common products or in social institutions and judge whether desired goals in a described situation have been achieved. This is associated with 'putting your finger on the problem', 'posing the right question' and 'getting straight to the crux of the matter'.

■ **Responses are judged to be clever**. This is a subjective evaluation, but there is usually significant agreement between judges in experiments. The same applies when a society or group agrees generally about a certain person's innate ability. This characteristic gets close to 'intelligence', but in the sense of 'sharp' or 'astute' rather than intellectually or cerebrally clever.

■ **Redefinition** – gives up old interpretations of familiar objects and uses them in new ways. For example, 'Which of the following objects could best be used to make a needle: pencil, radish, shoe, fish, carnation?' (fish – use bone).

■ **Elaboration** – can fill in details given a general scheme. For example: given a general task, will fill in the detailed steps. Given two simple lines, will draw a more complex object.

- **Tolerance of ambiguity** – willingness to accept some uncertainty in conclusions, not using rigid categories. Some creative people seem to be actually attracted to risk and uncertainty.
- **Interest in convergent thinking** – thinking towards one right answer, as in solving a mathematical problem stated in a textbook. Rather than 'left-brain' thinking, which is sometimes linked to a blinkered approach, this is the ability to focus on detail when necessary. British one-time Prime Minister Margaret Thatcher was able to concentrate on small details then immediately switch to global affairs. Quality thinking does not involve 'either or' but 'both', as we saw in the left–right brain distinction.
- **Interest in divergent thinking** – open-ended thinking, where there is not a single right answer. This feature is universally associated with creative thinking and forms a large part of the psychometric instruments.
- **Willing to be different and to defy convention.** This suggests a leader rather than a follower, but more in the sense of a leader in ideas rather than of people. The dislike of 'authority' applies to inanimate scientific laws and principles and rules generally as much as to hierarchical authority.
- **High self-discipline.** This is another example of the conscious thinking involved in the total creative process, in contrast to the often-cited unconscious aspects. Even self-discipline may be based on commitment to a task or domain, and may not apply in the absence of a motivating challenge.
- **High standards of excellence.** Self-measurement is also linked to self- or intrinsic motivation. Self-standards will increase as bigger challenges are pursued. The pursuit of excellence *per se* seems to be part of the person's motivation.
- **Willingness to take risks.** The form of risk will not be so much a gambling instinct as the risk of *failing* in diffi-

cult tasks with unknown outcomes. There are also risks in going a against popular opinion and 'received wisdom'.

These, taken from different studies of which many have been replicated, have been found to be common properties of creative individuals. Even though they have dominated the study of creativity, on reflection these observable mental characteristics and abilities are only a small part of wide definitions of creativity we met earlier. Much more important, it seems, are other factors seen in the geniuses of history:

- ■ motivation;
- ■ dedication to a particular domain;
- ■ 'living the work';
- ■ some luck in childhood;
- ■ early success in the chosen field;
- ■ being in a particular culture at a particular time in which others recognize a person's creativity.

CQ questions and commitments

Once you accept that you have all the innate creative resources you need, from a practical point of view it is also important to identify the barriers to creativity. These can be expressed as simple questions that are not too hard to answer but may help you to pitch your present CQ as high, middling or low. Fear of many things prevents us from being creative (see the diagram opposite).

You can turn these around, and express some of the characteristics in this chapter in simple, positive terms. To think creatively you must:

- ■ believe something can be done;
- ■ open your mind to new ideas;
- ■ aim to work smarter rather than harder;
- ■ make a habit of asking why;

- become more curious;
- stretch your mind;
- not get into a rut;
- make time to think;
- take the opposite view;
- see things from other points of view.

If you are below par in any of these respects, it requires a simple acknowledgement of the fact and commitment to change. The process may have already started as you learn about your brain resources and natural powers of creative thinking.

We can learn a lot from highly creative people, but we can also learn from what anybody does when they are being creative and this is where extensive psychometric and other research saves us a lot of effort. As well as understanding creative people and their traits, we can also learn about the mental processes they use, whether they realize it or not. Creative processes are the subject of the next chapter.

5

Creative processes

What do you *do* to be creative? Many people doubt their innate talents but will gladly follow a prescribed process. A lot of research on creativity has concerned the creative process, rather than, say, the personality of creative people that we covered in the previous chapter. This is an attractive approach for anyone interested in self-development, and the idea of a process also lends itself to company training programmes. There are different ways to address the creativity process, including the basic biological and psychological processes, such as the two-sided brain processing we met in Chapter 3. Many of the techniques you will meet in the final chapter try to capture known processes of divergent, or creative, thinking. In fact it is not always possible to distinguish between a process and a state, so this chapter looks at creativity only loosely from the point of view of processes.

Some processes are more directly useful than others, in particular if they lend themselves to simple techniques or skills you can master. Most people wouldn't worry about whether their creativity happened in the right or left side of the brain if they could turn it on on demand and maybe use it to get a better job or solve a personal problem. Others are more interested in what they can produce, such as new products and services, writing a book, a great invention or academic recognition, rather than the workings of either the psychological processes of the mind or the neurophysiological processes of the brain.

However, each approach to creative processes helps us to understand what creativity *is*. It offers another perspective on what we know is a complex and elusive concept. Even though other approaches seem to be coming from very different perspectives, a process may help to show how you can personally become more creative, or at least get started. The more you understand your own creativity, the more creative you will become. As with getting to know any subject in depth, the more you discover, the more motivated you are to improve your knowledge and skills still further. Understanding some of the basic processes of creative thinking in this chapter is another way to increase your CQ.

Divergent thinking

Research into the creative process psychologically has largely concerned divergent thinking, which we met earlier. This approximates the way we think creatively, or the mental process we use, although the simple term 'process' hardly reflects what happens in the brain. The popular creativity tests major on divergent thinking, applying its characteristics in the type of questions. For example, individuals are required to produce several responses to a specific prompt, in contrast to convergent thinking tests which require a single, correct answer – as with school and IQ tests. The main divergent thinking characteristic measured, although not the only one, is 'ideational fluency'. That usually means the number of eligible (not nonsense) responses to a 'prompt' question, like things to do with a brick.

Creativity tests (some are covered in Chapter 11) mirror the different processes involved in divergent thinking. These are fairly easily translated into questionnaire-type measurement tests. For example:

- ■ 'instances', such as thinking of as many things as you can that move on wheels;
- ■ 'semantic units', such as listing the consequences of not needing to sleep;

- ▧ figural classes – finding as many sets or classifications of figures as possible;
- ▧ figural units, such drawing as many objects as possible from basic geometric shapes.

These tests are fine for practice, just as maths problems are good for honing your left brain skills. And the categories of question are simple enough for you to design your own, and stretch yourself. To practise *Instances Test* exercises, for example, you can think of as many things as possible that: rattle, slide, click, drop, kick, swell, turn inside out and so on. You could pick verbs randomly from the dictionary. That may not solve a current problem, but it may help in the future just when you need it (like those screws, cloth and odds and ends you keep just in case). In any case, the mental exercise makes you mentally fit so that you have a sporting chance when real problems arise. Another plus is that any purposeful divergent thing done in this way adds to your mental database, so what may seem trivial in isolation may produce valuable ideas sooner.

A so-called *Uses Test* may require responses to prompts of the popular 'List all the different ways you could use a brick/matchstick etc' kind. If you are not into 'pretend' exercises, for 'uses' stick to *actual* things in the garage and loft that you have not got round to throwing out. That way you are more likely to produce creative products of value, and the whole exercise will be more realistic. When you find yourself thinking divergently as a habit, you know that you are boosting your CQ fast and making better use of your brain.

Other tests include word association, embedded figures, finishing off a story, construction tasks, pattern and line interpretation and so on. These set out to reflect the kinds of creative processes we use in the real world, except that we don't fill in questionnaires all the time. They are all examples of divergent thinking processes – a big part of your CQ. Here are a couple of well-known tests. If you've seen them before you just need memory, not divergent thinking:

Count the squares

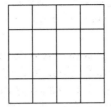

Join the dots with no more than four straight lines:

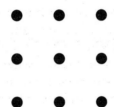

Suggested answers are given later in the book.

There is no standard creativity measure so you won't get a certificate for your new thinking skills. But the sorts of questions in tests are fine for mental practice. Better than external recognition, you will notice the difference in your life and start to get more pleasure out of what you do. Once you start to think divergently – turning things on their head, seeing things from other points of view, always looking for a better answer – you will find plenty of opportunities in everyday activities, however mundane they seemed in the past.

States and stages

The process of creativity has frequently been described as a sequential series of operations or stages, of which the following is typical:

These are familiar stages. Think about them in terms of the dual thinking processes you met in Chapter 3 about the brain. At first glance the first and last stages call for left-brain processing while the middle two call for right-brain processing. However, we saw that in practice all our thinking is holistic, and any hemispherical bias is just a matter of degree, and the way the brain does different things in parallel. For example, preparation usually includes problem definition, making assumptions, and maybe analysis. Each of these may require creative thinking, such as redefining the problem and interpreting any analysis. Likewise, the last stage is rarely plain, routine sailing. All sorts of obstacles may lie between a bright idea and its final realization, and any of these will require creative thinking whenever it crops up in a task or project.

Frustration

I add a 'frustration' stage before incubation. Usually we are ready to put something out of our mind when we hit a brick wall or find we are getting nowhere. The problem or task is getting too complex. That is the stage at which the incubation seems to happen and produce the eurekas. Almost all creative people go through such swings of emotion and have learnt to accept them as part of the process. By including frustration as a normal stage you will not be unduly bothered when it happens. In one sense it seems the unconscious mind just takes over when the conscious mind admits it has gone as far as it can. It is a strange sort of partnership.

An indication of the frustration stage is that the incubation stage does not work to order. In other words, just taking a break from a task doesn't mean that you will start an unconscious process that results in a spontaneous insight at some time.

Rather, it seems to follow a process of deep deliberation and 'mulling things over' – the sort of thinking we might do before going off to sleep with a worrying problem. This is the situation in which you are likely to wake up with an answer. It is part of the preparation stage in the classical thinking-stages model.

The rule therefore is: do what you can *consciously*, before sending the problem 'underground' for special treatment. It is another example of the sophisticated left–right brain partnership.

Uptime and downtime

Whilst the thinking stages model describes the overall creative process, different stages involve more or less divergent thinking – or right-brain thinking when expressed biologically. They also involve different levels of arousal, or consciousness, on a continuum. Incubation, or 'sleeping on a problem', by definition happens unconsciously, whereas some aspects of preparation and elaboration will be highly conscious. The continuum is sometimes referred to as going from uptime (conscious, focused, alert) to downtime (trance-like, unfocused). In the extreme it goes from sleep (in fact, coma) to being highly alert and aware of your external environment, such as in a job interview. The two ends of the continuum reflect the holistic and detail, right and left brain processes. The continuous movement up and down the scale, like the volume slider on a hi-fi, is illustrated in the continual switching between convergent and divergent thinking in the different thinking stages above.

Uptime

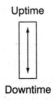

Downtime

You need to be in uptime when giving your attention to what is happening around you, such as when having an important conversation or when driving in heavy traffic in bad weather. However, much of our time we 'go inside', such as when thinking about something when driving so that we don't remember a whole chunk of a journey. This is typical downtime. It happens on a routine journey such as to work, or a boring motorway drive of one uneventful mile after the other. However, the slightest sign of danger ahead on the road, the sound of a police car, a sudden knocking from under the bonnet, or a name on the radio that somehow 'connects', will bring you instantly to uptime. Once the alarm is over, you may settle back down into comfortable, downtime freewheeling mode.

Paradoxically, you can be highly focused in downtime just as in uptime. This is akin to a hypnotic or trance state, in which you remove unwanted thoughts from your mind and focus on one thing. Thus when daydreaming, your world of memory or fantasy may be a lot more real to you than the boring lecture, or even busy airport lounge you wake up to. We met the downtime alpha brain state in Chapter 3.

The downtime state is particularly associated with creativity. It is the state we endeavour to induce by relaxation in order to recall specific memories or visualize something vividly, whether geographically distant or in the future. It is the state in which things are mentally 'sorted out'. Children often adopt this state and can 'become' anything. But many adults also find it easy to be oblivious to everything around. Although the time is not always used for *productive* creativity, the skill is well practised. Readers who cannot turn off in this way simply need to start practising moving further down the uptime–downtime ladder.

Going downtime

To get into downtime you need a period of uninterrupted time to yourself. You need not be alone, but your mind will probably not shut down to the here and now if it thinks you will be interrupted. Hence you can probably go inside easily in a busy place far from home where you are unlikely to be interrupted, but would probably incline to uptime in a less busy public place nearer home where you might be known and interrupted. Ordinary distractions like noise need not be a problem. We are all very different in this respect and it is also a matter of creative habits – which can be acquired by practice. Thus, if you are in the habit of playing background music you will tend to find a sudden silence an interruption, and it will bring you into uptime. Another person will respond the opposite way and the same sound causes arousal. People who commute to work by train for a few years often find that they can concentrate on what they are reading whatever is happening around them, whereas before they commuted they would find that other people's conversations interfered with what they were doing.

Going inside

'Going inside' is one of the main creativity foundational skills and is well worth perfecting (there is more on this in Chapter 14). You can *always* improve – and that applies to *any* mental process. The basic idea is to control your many mental states, including the basic sliding relationship between uptime and downtime. The various stages of creativity we met earlier involve a continuous shifting up and down the continuum. Even a cursory inner reflection or memory recollection during a conversation demands fast switches and we are all expert at this without realizing just how good we are. Eye movements during a conversation indicate when the person is going 'inside', say to consider a question or remember or imagine something. This is an example of the moment-by-moment state swings we all experience. However, you can adopt the skill for more specific creative tasks and aims, in particular entering extended downtime, trance-like periods when you can focus for as long as the challenge requires and do real business in your mind.

The biological process of creativity

A lot of work has been done on the biological processes affecting creativity. This has been helped by advances in computer-enhanced scanning technology. Brain activity can be observed while a subject is carrying out different kinds of mental task. We have come a long way from feeling phrenological bumps on people's heads.

Arousal

Creativity has been associated with cortical arousal, which is another manifestation of the uptime–downtime continuum. Arousal extends from sleep through alert wakefulness to states of emotional tension. Learning and optimal performance are related to *medium* levels of arousal, following a U-shaped curve. Paradoxically, ignoring extremes, simple tasks are performed best at high states of arousal, whereas more complex tasks that demand divergent, or 'lateral' thinking are best done at low brainwave levels. Low levels of arousal are associated with high levels of slow, alpha brainwave recordings, which in turn correlate to greater creativity. The period just before going off to sleep exemplifies the alpha state and is a particularly productive time for creative thinking. Your body is relaxed and your brain ticks over slowly yet is alert and open to suggestion, vivid visualization and distant memory recall. Similarly, a trance-like reverie state is creatively productive.

The main biological focus of research is hemispherical activity – in the respective right and left sides of the brain. As would be expected from the kinds of operations that each side does best (Chapter 3), scans show activity, or cortical arousal, in the right side when divergent thinking takes place. As we saw, to some degree the *whole brain* remains active when 'resting', or between behaviours, as though poised in anticipation for the next, most likely sensory event. This confirms the holistic, or whole-brain nature of the thinking process.

Focus

We know little about creativity from a biological perspective, just as we have reached no conclusions about the biological basis of consciousness and self – the other great elusive psychological concepts. But what we do know is useful metaphorically. For example, the right brain is associated with an holistic, overall 'forest' view whereas the left brain is associated with a close-up, component part, detailed or 'tree' perspective. The bicameral, or twin-sided, aspects of thinking – and indeed creativity – can be seen in just about any sphere of behaviour, whether traditionally considered to be creative or not. In other words, every behaviour has both a detail, or focused, aspect and at the same time a more holistic, defocused aspect. The analogy is seeing both the tree and the forest rather than just either, incomplete perspective.

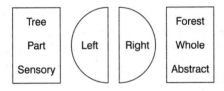

Given the fact that the whole brain works in concert, we can, however, observe on scans where activity is dominant. The left-brain activity especially can be traced to distinct regions, as the close neural firing is more localized. Hence the left-brain regions responsible for language and speech have been known for many years from brain injuries affecting those sites, and these are reconfirmed graphically by scans.

Localized processing

Scanning has revealed localization in some very specific aspects of vision and language. The whole body's sensory motor systems are mirrored in an equivalent brain mapping on the opposite side of the brain. Many of the findings affect tasks we associate with creativity. As we saw in Chapter 3, some brain centres involved with music production, for example, are in the right hemisphere, as is the case with visual arts.

There is also evidence that the right brain is more involved with visualized internal images – the stuff of creative thinking – than is the left. Wilder Penfield's famous experiments found that stimulating the right cortex produced very realistic childhood memory recall, such that the patients thought they were actually reliving the experience. It seemed as though a complete memory recording was lodged in the brain's neuronal networks, accessible only through the unconscious mind. We get a glimpse of this in deep reverie and dreams.

There is evidence that procedures for increasing right-brain activation can increase creativity. Similarly, in the case of highly hypnotizable subjects (the hypnotic or trance state is associated with 'downtime'), hypnosis increases right hemisphere activation.

The broad left- and right-brain distinction has been well established, even though some of the mechanisms of thought remain a mystery. But that is not the whole story. For example, whilst the left brain is well known to specialize in language, the right side has a lexicon of its own, although not grammatically arranged. The nuances of meanings in words, metaphor, humour and suchlike thrive in the right-brain imagination. A poet, for instance, might call on right-brain inspiration whilst handling language in its logical structure as a 'left-brain function'. Entirely different mental processes are at work in these different dimensions of thought. Harnessing these more consciously and specifically is a key to creativity.

Creative people do not show different brain function in a *resting* state, when compared with non-creative people ('creative' as based on psychometric tests) but only when *carrying out* a creative task. So a creative *personality*, if such exists, has not been traced on a scan (nor to a 'creativity gene'). Moreover, a person demonstrates more right-brain activity when *asked to think creatively* (for example, in telling a story) than when not prompted to be creative. So, not only is the brain plastic in all its operations, but highly open to suggestion and information in whatever it does. As we saw in Chapter 3, nothing in the brain stands still, but a continuous cybernetic process is at work.

Interesting differences have been discovered between people of high, low and medium creativity based on standard creativity tests. Highly creative subjects showed more right-brain activity; those of medium creativity, strangely, showed the reverse asymmetry – more left-brain activity; while the low creativity subjects showed about equal activation. Left-brain activation is associated with conscious thought, and *trying*. That's when your brain seems to hurt. This may explain the paradox for the medium creativity group: they are creative enough to know they can be more creative and so *try harder*. Remember, of course, that the resting state shows more activation on the left side, so the *task* called upon equal increments of hemispherical brain activity. It could be that low creativity people, showing minimal right-brain bias, don't even 'try' to be creative in the way that moderately creative people do.

Laid-back learning

Paradoxically, highly creative people seem to take a relaxed approach to even the most complex problems and tasks. We have known the influence of relaxation on creativity and general well-being for a long time. Biologically, they generate low-frequency, alpha brainwaves. They are not hard-wired differently to others but they seem to *know* that trying harder doesn't help when you want a creative solution. We can all learn from this. You don't have to reinvent wheels to increase your CQ.

This does not mean that creative people have special brain control generally. It has been found that they do not outperform less creative people in biofeedback test final results, but that they do *learn more quickly*. It just means they somehow *know how to do it* when others have to be shown, and may require some practice. Nevertheless, with practice we can all achieve alpha state. That is one of the best learning investments, not just for creativity, but for all sorts of behavioural change through visualization and neuro-linguistic programming.

Creative people also show greater *variability* in arousal when carrying out a creative task with its above stages, moving up and down the uptime–downtime, attention–defocus continuum. Flexibility of brain state reflects the flexibility of thinking which is a key characteristic in most creativity models.

Soft and hard focus

Creativity is associated with defocused attention. To make associations and analogies, you have to think of more than one thing at the same time. Two things mean one potential relationship, analogy or new meaning; four things produce six; six produce thirteen; and so on. So we soon run out of conscious processing power. To think over novel associations, rather than *depth* of focus, you need *breadth* of focus – a holistic view that takes in the whole rather than parts. That requires what has been termed soft focus, rather than the hard focus we need to attend to the here-and-now external world. It means resorting to unconscious mental processes.

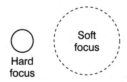

Non-creative people are not able to handle more than one or two concepts at the same time so do not have the fluency and flexibility of creative people. Hence the creative combination: low cortical arousal, or downtime; high levels of (slow) alpha brainwave frequency; wide rather than deep focus; right- as well as left-brain activity. The bicameral, 'forest-tree' thinking processes repeat themselves in every aspect of our thinking.

Inhibition

Research has shown that creativity decreases when a person is inhibited in some way. This may be:

▮ when observed;
▮ when aware they are being tested;
▮ when under authority;
▮ even when a reward is offered for successful completion of a task.

It seems paradoxical, therefore, that creative people love novelty, and the risks and uncertainty it brings. Along with this is an active *dislike* for things that are not novel, or a low threshold for routine and boredom. The English writer, George Moore, wrote: 'The commonplace, the natural, is constitutionally abhorrent', and the French poet Charles Baudelaire remarked that 'the beautiful is always bizarre'. More creative scientists also tend to harbour scepticism for traditional ideas and dogmas.

Better brainstorming

Inhibition takes many forms, including the presence of other people, and this has an interesting bearing on brainstorming as a technique. Contrary to decades of practice, it has been shown that brainstorming may actually *decrease* creativity, merely because of the presence of others. Of course, the greater number of people can account for the volume (as distinct from quality) of ideas generated, as can the social stimulation of less creative people who perform better in a group. There is more on brainstorming as a technique in Chapter 14.

Many people like to be on their own when concentrating on complex tasks, however, sometimes for long periods, and can produce prodigious quantities of ideas. This is a feature of highly creative people historically, such as inventors and research scientists. Creative people are 'physiologically reactive' and have a lower resistance to outside stimuli, in some cases including pain. For instance, they respond more than non-creative people to electric shocks and noise. They are sensitive.

This helps to explain the effect of 'inhibitors' such as being watched, or thinking about rewards and other motivators during the creative process. Even non-creative people, once they get started on their own, will produce as many or more ideas than in a group, where 'air-time' is limited anyhow, and the more extro-vert members of the group tend to dominate. Thus when compared with individual divergent thinking, group brainstorm-ing loses hands down. Team interaction is required in various ways, of course, and will usually have a positive rather than negative effect outside the specially sensitive area of creativity.

There is an important distinction that helps to explain the different effects of arousal from person to person: creative people tend to seek *mental* stimulation rather than the excite-ment of real-world adventure. That doesn't require outside motivators such as material rewards, nor the stimulation of other people such as in a team. Mental self-motivation is the best way to be independent of authority and outside constraints, factors known to inhibit creativity.

The flow process

Mihaly Csikszentmihalyi in his book *Flow: The Psychology of Happiness* described the state of 'flow'. This is a period of optimal behaviour, or mastery, during which a person achieves high levels of output and pleasure in the process with little conscious effort. It happens in every sphere of life, from sport, art and music to a routine process in the factory or spring-clean-ing the house. It is accompanied by a sense of well-being and high self-esteem. Such times are unpredictable, but often happen either at work when a task provides its own pleasure and moti-vation, or in an area in which the person has above-average knowledge and skill and a special interest. Like all creative processes, it is also related to intrinsic motivation.

The path to happiness

Flow happens at a point when the level of perceived challenge or difficulty of a task is balanced by a person's perceived ability to carry it out. It usually involves a challenge or 'stretching'. A person will therefore continually require higher challenges to achieve the same level of flow. It happens in a path steered between boredom on the one hand (because a task is not stimulating or complex enough), and over-anxiety on the other (because of the fear of not being able to do it).

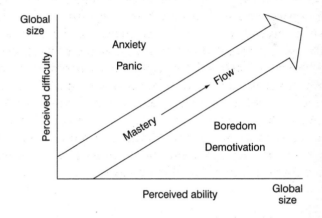

This optimal exertion and challenge can apply to a jogger improving her time by a few seconds, a musician perfecting an arrangement he had not managed to conquer, or doing any sort of complex task a little better or faster than previously achieved. There can be a sense of elation so great that the flow state becomes addictive, and the person seeks ever-larger and riskier (the risk of failure) challenges.

The perceived challenge also affects a person's 'ideational fluidity', or the number of different possible solutions that they generate – another feature of creativity. This key relationship between the perceived task and our perceived ability varies from person to person, of course, as well as from task to task. It also changes over the months and years as we grow in experience, skills and confidence based on past successes. It helps to explain why a highly creative person, such as a research scientist, inclines towards either a new domain or some obscure or controversial aspect of their present domain – they run out of challenges. On the other hand, applying a challenge to a routine activity such as production-line work or repetitive clerical work – such as continuously reducing the time it takes – can create the same flow process. Time flies and the work seems effortless and pleasurable.

The Muse

The flow experience is highly correlated to creativity, and creative products often arise during such periods. For example, a piece of prose will seem to write itself, or a hitherto intractable problem will seem to disappear as the mind effortlessly overcomes one obstacle after another. However, a flow experience usually occurs in the context of a conscious, complex or problematic task in a domain very familiar to the person, rather than as a single, spontaneous insight unconnected with present behaviour. Unlike the classical sudden insight, flow can extend to many hours, but it can end as suddenly as it started. Such experiences are especially prone to interruptions, and therefore usually happen when the person is alone. A creative person learns to 'shut off' mentally and avoid interruptions.

The flow experience has been associated with famous historical figures who composed music, wrote books and poems, unravelled scientific problems or perfected an invention. However, it is something that ordinary people from every culture are very familiar with, even though the experience might happen more rarely and at a different level of expertise. Like any creative experience, flow can be stimulated by creating the right conditions. Immersing yourself deeply and long enough in a specialized sphere of knowledge or skill, in which you have high intrinsic motivation, will usually create regular, although still unpredictable flow experiences. It helps to keep a creativity journal or find space in your diary to record these. More frequent flow 'events' are a sure sign of an increased creativity quotient.

Flow characteristics

Descriptions of flow differ, and different terms are used such as 'in the zone', 'on a high', 'on a roll' and suchlike. However, the main characteristics seem to apply universally.

Effort

Unlike creative insights that arise spontaneously, flow is linked to real effort – albeit a special kind of effort. Sometimes it is accompanied by long periods of intensive work and deprivation of food and sleep. However, invariably the person suffers no pain or displeasure and typically loses all track of time. In other words, subjectively there is little conscious effort at all. If there is, it is a pleasurable *plus* rather than a negative factor. Usually time 'just disappears', as in a period of daydreaming. At other times a brief moment – such as a dance manoeuvre or a stroke in sport – can seem endless or to happen in slow motion. The senses seem heightened and you may remember such times in vivid detail for many years.

Event

Flow does not seem to fit the conventional creative process that involves different stages and includes a period of incubation and a moment of inspiration. It is more like an extended event than a process. Flow just has a start and a finish – although these may merge imperceptibly into a normal period of work. However, invariably there will be a creative product, and the person will have something to show for such special times. The product may be an idea, a 'personal best' in a sport, pastime or artistic or musical performance, a successfully completed task, or just a surge of energy, productivity and pleasure in the moment. That is, the experience is productive as seen by the person.

Enjoyment

Flow may reflect a person's personality and be almost a way of life, such as to enjoy each moment, or take risks. It is not like a gift or genetic talent such as musical or artistic ability, which is a more predictable skill consciously performed. For the period in question, flow reflects a particular and somewhat special state of mind, but also an enjoyable, memorable, sometimes protracted event or behaviour.

The quality of flow varies, of course. The level of skill at which a person operates, its intensity or uniqueness will vary, just as flashes of inspiration vary in the impact they make and their value. The value of a flow experience will also depend on the very different nature of the activities involved, from cleaning out the garage to composing a symphony.

Ideas

External behaviour need not be involved, and a flow experience may just involve a flow of ideas that result in a solution to a problem, an invention, a mathematical or scientific principle, a plot for a novel or whatever might happen entirely in the mind. In that case, the person can usually immediately record in detail their insights, as if dictated from outside, or seen on a screen to simply transcribe. Or they might recall what they experienced afterwards like remembering a vivid dream, and record it while it is fresh. In other words, it is not only a real 'product' from the person's point of view, but is potentially of value in a wider, cultural context. In this case flow is like extended 'inspiration' in the thinking stages model.

Universal flow

The flow process seems to happen universally. It supports the notion that we are all naturally creative. The difference between us and well-known genius figures – who have more or less the same physical brain – is a matter of degree, kind, quality and frequency. For example:

- ▓ The different levels at which we operate, such as in the difference between flow in a weekend football match or in a World Cup game.
- ▓ The kind of creative products the flow experience produces: a scientific breakthrough can change all our lives, and a virtuoso musical performance can capture the emotions of thousands of people.
- ▓ The quality of the experience. Reading a good book can provide a pleasurable flow experience, but may not be of the quality to conceive the plot as an author and draft it in detail in one sitting. There will come a point, of course, at which quantity of reasonable quality is more useful than high but rare quality – life is too short.
- ▓ The frequency with which these experiences occur. The rarity of flow experiences has a more pragmatic explanation: most people have allowed their childlike imagination to atrophy through neglect and cultural conditioning.

The universality of the flow experience offers an important resource. Using neuro-linguistic programming methods, you can recall such experiences, replicate the *states* and utilize them in areas of your life that you do not associate with creativity. For example, a person may be quite familiar with such times when playing a sport such as golf, yet they do not apply their mental programme to solving work or domestic problems. A major difference seen in highly creative people is that they actively *seek out* flow experiences, or psychological highs (whatever they call them). Some seem almost addicted to the continuing higher challenges and successes. They in effect practise the *skill* of being creative. They enjoy it, so do it more and in so doing get even better. Practising creative processes helps perfect them.

Instant eurekas

This doesn't mean that you ever reach the stage where you can turn on a flow state, or call up an immediate eureka. The process doesn't happen in that way. It does mean, however, that such special times will be more frequent, and that you will build the confidence in your ability to carry out future tasks successfully. Such an attitude is self-fulfilling, of course (just like a negative self-belief and worry), and is a very powerful resource when faced with otherwise impossible situations.

From what little we know of the flow process, for practical purposes we can put forward some fundamental approaches to increasing our personal creativity:

- Do what you enjoy.
- Broaden your mind with new experiences and information.
- Immerse yourself in the task in hand.
- Don't try to force flow, but be very thankful for it when it comes.

Flow experiences are some of the most fruitful and memorable times we as humans can enjoy. They seem to be at the heart of what it means to be uniquely human. They can make you a hundredfold more productive. They can turn what might have been a laborious, unrewarding task into something you would pay to do. A single flow experience can mean a quantum advance in personal development, or a turning point in your life. We do not know the neurophysiology of such experiences, but that does not stop you from enjoying them (just like electricity at the flick of a switch) once you know how to programme the process into your life.

6

Creative products

How do we shape a novel thought into something of quality and value – something useful? Once we agree on a creative 'product' – maybe something tangible like a painting, sculpture or labour-saving gadget – creativity gets easier to define and measure. It also lends itself to scientific research. The products usually cited are patents, works of art and music, new consumer products and suchlike. To the individual, of course, an idea is a creative product, and a 'great idea' clearly has value. In wanting to be more creative you need to decide what creative 'products' you intend to produce.

What makes a creative product?

It's not quite that straightforward, or the mystery would have gone out of creativity a long time ago. To start with, defining creativity in terms of creative products just raises the question of how we define a creative product. The ones I have quoted seem obvious cases to illustrate this dilemma. Insofar as they are measurable, they are useful for research into creativity generally. But they do not represent the myriad of productive outcomes of human creativity.

Quality vs. quantity

Take patents. There is a great difference between filing a patent and inventing an ingenious, top-selling new product or process. The patent is no more than legal protection against copying. In the same way, there is a great difference between a large number of patents that never proceed to development and the market-place, and a handful (in the name of another, less prolific person) that result in successful real products, or indeed a single world-beater like the vacuum cleaner or Walkman. We met the quality vs. quantity dilemma when considering the different values of a creative insight or flow experience.

This raises the question, not just of the difference between quantity and quality when it comes to creativity, but of who decides. A truly creative inventor may be decades ahead, not just of the market, but of his or her contemporary inventors. In many cases creative ideas were ahead of the technology to turn them into reality, and they were picked up later. Besides, you need ingenuity, commercial acumen, communication skills or whatever to translate a creative idea into a profitable product. But are these other skills particularly creative? Or is that what we *mean* by creativity? Or does the creativity lie in the idea itself? We are no nearer answering such questions today, but they do highlight the need to identify creativity in terms of the 'products' created.

A work of art or music might, on the face of it, provide a simpler illustration of a creative product. People go to an art gallery to see a picture, or pay big money to buy it, and buy CDs or go to a concert hall to listen to music. However, there can often be a long time gap between the creation of a work and its acceptance by the public as a product they will pay money for or travel to a gallery in the rain to look at. In some cases the artist is long since dead. In other cases many years elapse before the artist's name is sufficiently well known to gain the necessary exposure to a potential audience. That's a publishing, marketing or public relations function. It calls on creativity, but not in the way we usually associate with the creative person or work of art itself.

Value and vogue

Modern art, especially of the controversial love–hate sort, illustrates the dilemma more than anything. Say the work of art is a cow chopped in half. The fact that thousands process past it in a leading national gallery, on the face of it, attests to its status as a 'creative product'. But where does the creativity lie? Or more specifically, what part of the marketing package does the *creative* product comprise? The butchery skills? The publicity and PR? The display, lighting and setting? Or the idea itself? If the latter, do I simply have to think of crazy ideas to become a creative person? That being the case, a person who tends to remember their dreams will beat a non-dreamer hands down, and a child of under five will have little competition from adults. Schizophrenics might corner the artistic market. Creativity has always had some connotations of madness and eccentricity.

New products are no easier to tie down to a creative label. In the case of the Walkman, or the Dyson vacuum cleaner, the real creativity is in the invention, of course, rather than in the long process to eventual mass distribution of the final physical product. But these historical innovations are the exceptions. Thousands of new products every year are for the most part repackaged or slightly improved versions of the same thing. Moreover, in the present corporate world many individuals are likely to contribute to ideas, decisions and the chain of events that create the product that the public decides to buy. Even in the scientific world, although we associate one or two individuals with significant discoveries, it may be the luck of the draw who actually gets the credit in the history books (it varies from country to country anyway). So in considering creative products we are faced with the same difficulty of definition, before we ever attempt to measure a product's value and the creativity quotient of its creator.

Novelty and usefulness

Clearly 'product' can extend to an idea, or non-material product – something in the mind where the idea came from. Patents, which are used a lot in research when measuring the relative creativity of different people, are simply the recorded 'ideas' – or intellectual property. But, just as obviously, any old bizarre notion or childish imagining will not qualify. It seems, therefore, that the criteria for a creative product are no different from the twin criteria for creativity: novelty and usefulness. Novelty is more likely to be present than usefulness, and may extend to nonsense fantasy. Having said that, few works of art, music or literature have not been partially based on somebody else's idea, or a major influence outside the creator. What is new under the sun?

Usefulness is another matter altogether. It may be implicit in the need for patent protection, the willingness of the public to buy a product, or view a work of art. But usefulness and value are at best extremely subjective concepts. Does the auction value of a work of art equate to its creative worth? Likewise, crowds flock to see a celebrity singing artiste, but it may be hard to tie down the motive to anything of *value*, other than fame or notoriety. Usefulness implies value – but value to whom? The buying public or punter, or the creative person him or herself? These are academic questions until you want to be creative personally and you want to know on what basis your creative products will be measured.

Products and purpose

For the person who wants to be more creative the idea of creative product is vital. It is what you want to do, get or achieve. One or more of your hierarchy of goals should be fulfilled through your creative product. Creativity doesn't happen in a vacuum. It follows some purpose or other. In partic-ular, the spontaneous eureka flashes of inspiration most associ-ated with right-brain creativity don't come from nowhere. They reflect the desires and intentions already somewhere in your mind. Although they may be triggered by something you see or hear in the world outside (like a falling apple or water overflowing from a bath tub), the creativity is in the association with something already waiting for a solution or an opportunity – something you may have been pondering for a long time. So inner goals, dreams, intentions and desires are not wasted, even when for the moment you cannot see the pathway to a goal or the solution of a problem.

Inner products

The more real, or lifelike, the inner goal or desire, the more chances of getting a creative 'hit'. In other words, the more likelihood of an association with one or more of the billions of sensory inputs we process day by day (most pass into the ether unnoticed). So the creative 'product' is the imagined outcome of your creativity. It exists before it ever becomes reality, and it cannot become reality without first being conceived in your mind.

When it comes to a spontaneous insight, the product – to the creative person – may be the moment the conscious mind receives it. Before that it did not *exist* (in consciousness). Some definitions of creativity stop there. But creative people usually want to express their creativity, such as in words, music, art or a physical product. In every case, the product starts in the mind as a multi-sensory image.

The power of a clear, visualized intention is good news for personal creativity. It means that you can influence your level of creativity, or increase your CQ, *just by imagining*. What you focus on tends to bring up the vital, creative associations and mental analogies. Buy a new Audi and suddenly Audis are everywhere. There is meaning in things you suddenly notice or in sudden ideas: your mind acts on purpose. But creativity doesn't stop at an ingenious association. You can convert your creativity into real goals and accomplishments. In other words, get what you want out of life.

To help boost your CQ, when thinking 'creative', think *product*. It focuses the mind and adds the important 'appropriate' qualification to your originality. And the creative product need not be a patent or a great work of art. The product is what you want in your life, in the short, medium and long term. It is *getting* what you want, *doing* what you want and – most importantly – *being* the person you want to be. You can create a sense of well-being, meaning in your life, purpose and so on. You can create a better job, better relationships, a better home and environment and so on. Human creativity is neither trivial nor mysterious, and nor need it be the rare privilege of the few. Potentially we all possess the creativity usually associated with genius or special gifts. For one thing, we all have more or less the same brain, and that's where it happens. You can physically improve your brain by using it more and in the right way, and thus adding new synaptic networks. You can also stimulate and harness the creative side of your brain, such as by multi-sensory focusing on goals, relaxing, 'incubating' problems and so on. This part of your brain was previously thought to be out of conscious reach, and part of serendipity or luck. You can even create an environment amenable to creative thoughts, just as some successful companies have done at a corporate level. In short, creating creative products is very much in your own hands.

7

Intelligence and creativity

Intelligence is no easier to define than creativity. 'She's intelligent', 'she's smart', or 'she's a bright cookie' may mean no more than 'she agrees with me!' Piaget said intelligence is what you use when you don't know what to do. Maybe creativity is what you need when intelligence doesn't work either.

Some definitions of intelligence include creativity, but no popular definitions of creativity include intelligence, even though creativity – like intelligence – spreads its 'characteristics' net wide. Creativity and intelligence obviously relate in some way, but any relationship depends on which characteristics or personal traits you include within each respectively – and how you define them.

Theories about the relationship between intelligence and creativity are as legion as the definitions of the terms. Creativity is commonly seen as a subset of intelligence, or at the extreme is off the scale and excluded altogether. At the other extreme, intelligence is a subset of creativity. In between, they are seen to overlap, perhaps as part of a three-circle relationship with another factor, such as motivation.

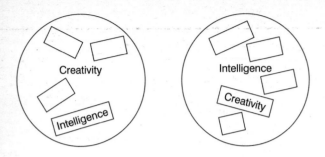

Or they are seen to be two quite different things.

Even more extreme is the view that creativity 'doesn't exist' and is just a feature of problem solving. All the main theories can sound convincing, but the dominant conclusion seems to be that creativity and intelligence are related but only partially, and that it depends what you mean in both cases anyway.

IQ and CQ

When comparing IQ scores and scores on various creativity instruments, there is no correlation between the two above a certain level of intelligence (about 120 IQ). In other words, high IQ people are not necessarily highly creative. Most of us would have guessed that from our own acquaintances. There is some correlation, however, between low IQ and low creativity. Below-average IQ people are not well represented among very creative people. Highly creative people tend to be of *average or above average* intelligence, and according to the 'threshold' theory the positive correlation (the relationship is never negative) stops at about an IQ of 120. However, these correlations are based on IQ-type 'intelligence' which is considered to be predictive in certain areas only, such as academic performance, and doesn't hold good outside the culture in which the test is designed. In other words, it doesn't measure overall intelligence any better than creativity tests measure creativity.

Does this mean that low IQ people are doomed to a low CQ? On the contrary. To start with, you can increase your IQ if you care to. My book *Boost Your Intelligence* covers that specifically. More to the point, you can certainly be more creative, just as you can increase your emotional intelligence (EQ). (That's in *Quick Fix Your Emotional Intelligence*.) These do not reflect genetic factors as IQ is supposed to. Creativity is an aspect of intelligence, so, boost your creativity and you boost your *true* intelligence. The fact that traditional IQ tests do not properly measure creativity is not your problem, and explains the fallacy of correlating a test that does not measure creativity with creativity. Even divergent thinking tests only capture creativity in some respects. This explains why there is no correlation between highly creative people and those with a high IQ. The correlation at the average level tells us that people who are averagely bright are usually also averagely creative. In other words, most of the population (around the mode) use both sides of their brain.

So you can be more creative and more intelligent into the bargain. It is a package that comes with using your whole brain more effectively, mostly through knowledge and know-how and practice (repetition). If you fancy having a higher IQ, get the other book, as a lot is to do with test familiarity – hence the cynical view that having a high IQ means being good at IQ tests.

Achievement and aptitude

Let us clear up a common misunderstanding. Intelligence doesn't mean achievement, which is the knowledge and skills acquired through experience and the 'success' it brings by putting your intelligence *into practice*. Nor does intelligence mean aptitude, which refers to a person's capability of acquiring knowledge or skills in a particular domain, such as maths or athletics. Intelligence reflects a person's ability to adapt to the environment in every aspect, rather than in just one or two domains. Creativity, in the same way, does not equate to achievement and aptitude, although it can easily be confused with aptitude and can certainly affect a person's achievement, or so-called creative products.

True intelligence is hard to measure, of course, although not so hard to *identify* as a quality or trait. It may apply to domains or skills a person has not even tried – 'She can put her hand to anything.' This is how we can see intelligence in children before they have been able to put it into practice. The same applies to creativity, which of course forms a larger part of children's intelligence before they start school and are groomed in IQ-type intelligence characteristics.

'Smart' usually means smart across the board. It *includes* the sort of intelligence that IQ tests measure, but a lot more. Moreover, as is argued in the case of EQ, those other types of intelligence – such as dealing with other people and being 'street-wise' – may be far more important for day-to-day living and 'success' in life generally.

Culture-based intelligence

A person scoring a high IQ probably exhibits aptitude (and no doubt related achievement) in verbal reasoning and numeracy, two main elements of the test, but not (necessarily) 'true' intelligence. Placed in a different culture and landscape, for instance, they may appear as singularly unintelligent to a native of the country and might not survive in a shanty town. Only a broader test of intelligence would measure both individuals fairly, and would need to include, for instance, 'hunting intelligence', 'weather intelligence' or 'getting along with neighbours intelligence', and other tests of a person's ability to 'adapt to the environment' – a key definition of intelligence. No such culture-free instrument has been designed. Not surprisingly, the aspects of intelligence that we have come to measure – especially in IQ tests which are still used widely – are those that are quite easy to measure and usually have a single answer. That is, they can at least be administered practically.

Furthermore, we are *conscious* of such ways of thinking, such as when making a logical deduction or doing an arithmetic calculation. Creativity, on the other hand, is more associated with the unconscious rather than conscious mind. It happens in different combinations of regions of the brain, and constitutes a different *kind* of holistic brain processing. Not only is it difficult to test 'unconscious' processes practically, but that kind of thought may not be measurable psychometrically at all. We address psychometrics in Chapter 11. CQ is not a metric concept like IQ, but a qualitative concept more like EQ, and is even less amenable to quantification in numbers.

Varieties of intelligence

Most definitions of intelligence include creativity in some form or other, but the emphasis varies a lot, and the term may not be used directly.

Multiple intelligences

Howard Gardner lists several 'intelligences' in his multiple intelligences theory. Creativity doesn't appear as such as one of his seven 'domains' other than implicitly in 'musical intelligence'. His intelligences comprise:

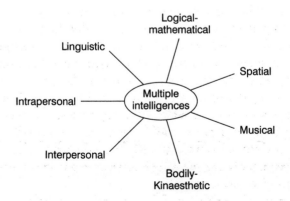

- linguistic intelligence – reading, writing and language;
- logical-mathematical intelligence – logical reasoning, mathematical abilities;
- spatial intelligence – reading maps and getting from place to place;
- musical intelligence – composing, singing, playing instruments, enjoying music;
- bodily-kinaesthetic intelligence – running, dancing, playing sports;
- interpersonal intelligence – understanding and relating to others; 'people' skills;
- intrapersonal intelligence – understanding oneself, dealing with personal issues.

Most of our education focuses on the first two domains – linguistic and logical-mathematical – although schools are increasingly using Gardner's model and trying to redress the intelligence balance.

None of these categories is weighted for relative importance, and the more we focus on components, the harder it is to understand the essence of intelligence, and where creativity might fit in. In any case, we usually refer to an intelligent person *as a person* rather than just as a musician, mathematician, dancer or whatever and the same applies to a 'creative person'. Hence we might describe a musical person not as a creative person but as a musical person.

Emotional intelligence

Creativity does not figure as such in EQ either, the concept popularized by Daniel Goleman in his book *Emotional Intelligence*. EQ emphasizes two of Gardner's domains: interpersonal and intrapersonal intelligence. The first relates to communication and 'people' skills; the second concerns self-understanding and knowing or communicating with oneself. All of Goleman's five domains of emotional intelligence address these inter (between) and intra (among) aspects of intelligence:

- knowing your emotions;
- managing your emotions;
- motivating yourself;
- recognizing emotions in others;
- handling relationships.

Like Howard Gardner's multiple intelligences, these are often compared with IQ-type intelligence to illustrate its limited application. However, the particular 'communication' (inner and outer) emphasis of the EQ model doesn't help when considering creativity any more than a list of intelligences like Gardner's. For example, is creativity just one of several intelligences (as we saw, the number of 'intelligences' in some models reaches to scores)? Or is creativity of a different order such that it affects all other components of intelligence in a way that the others don't? For example, could one exercise more or less creativity when displaying musical, linguistic or interpersonal intelligence? Consider, for example, the difference between:

- an outstanding extempore jazz musician and an experienced session musician;
- a poet or creative writer and a professional writer of technical prose;
- a naturally gifted therapist and a 'likeable' 'people person';
- a solo violinist and a professional orchestral violinist.

In the last case, is there something more than technical skill and experience that sets the up-front solo performer apart? More specifically, might a successful solo artist be less technically skilled than an unknown orchestral player? In such cases we would put their success down to a certain indefinable 'something'. In this sense creativity is a different kind of mental animal – something quite apart from intelligence in the sense that we understand the word.

Creative people skills

We can illustrate the distinction using the EQ component 'inter-personal intelligence', roughly described as communication or 'people' skills. A person may act exquisitely socially by express-ing themselves clearly, listening well, appearing interested, seeking to understand the other person's point of view, trying to gauge their emotions through what they say and their observ-able body language, and so on. A really nice person. They would score well on an EQ test, especially a self-administered one, as many are.

Someone else may not exhibit these characteristics so obvi-ously yet they have an uncanny ability to understand the other person, even when the person is covering their emotions well. It is as if they have an antenna that intuitively *feels* for the other person. For instance, such a person may know that something is wrong from the first few words of a telephone conversation. Or they somehow pick up nuances of body language that are invisi-ble to others. They have the ability to express their own feelings also, without doing it *consciously*. So they can communicate empathy even when they don't use the right words, or don't use any words. Yet their demeanour and outward appearance may not set them apart as an extrovert 'people person' like the high EQ person.

It is often hard to put your finger on what makes the person so effective in *outcomes* whatever process they adopt. Clearly, the difference happens in the brain and mostly unconsciously. Furthermore, the more creative communicator will probably also be creative in other parts of their life.

In fact both the above examples of interpersonal intelligence exhibit a degree of emotional intelligence, and – perhaps quite wrongly – would probably score similarly on a variety of tests. Many teachers, trainers and coaches never make it themselves to the top level in the skills that they teach. The significance here is not how these different categories of 'communicator' score on an interpersonal intelligence scale, but the fact that there is a fundamental difference in what is happening in their mind –

how they do what they do. One tends to act *consciously*, and can probably describe what they do when communicating (important in a teacher or coach, for example). The other acts more *unconsciously* and intuitively – she *doesn't know* how she knows, speaks and acts in a certain way.

The special 'something'

This sort of difference compares with the difference between 'smart', creative people as we know them and academically brainy people. It is as if they run a different computer operating system and both 'excel' but in different ways. In fact, in the extreme, they operate as two brains: left and right. A truly intelligent person is creative, and makes fuller use of *both* brains, *and the connecting fibres between them.* In other words, he or she thinks holistically.

This is a fundamentally different way of thinking. We observe it in every kind of achiever, such as scientists, architects, entrepreneurs, musicians, comedians, footballers, racing drivers and so on. It is the special creative, indefinable 'extra' seen in a few, but not many, in every walk of life and at every social stratum. In such cases the creative 'plus' is more than 'book' intelligence, which may be secondary to the unique creative gift, virtuosity or genius. That seems to be the case with many top artists with limited formal education. When you witness such people at close hand, it is easy to see how creativity has been considered separate from, and on another dimension to, ordinary intelligence.

In creativity research not many professors and top professionals rank with the 'high creatives'. Whatever their childhood propensities, both groups tend to be influenced by the 'left brain' institutions they serve. Nor are many high creatives found in the high-IQ echelons of Mensa. In this case left-brain dominance and a preponderance of symbolic intelligence (words and numbers) usually go back to successful conformity at school and college, and possibly some parental hot-housing pre-school. The difference in the two types of intelligence is often intuitively obvious (except to a heavily left-brain-dominant person) even though you can't define creative insight or translate it into a training manual.

This important distinction reflects the way the left and right sides of the brain operate, as we saw in Chapter 3: the left in a linear, logical, conscious way, with attention to 'parts' and detail; the right in a more holistic, intuitive, unconscious way that sees the big picture and underlying meaning. In this light, what we might call the 'creative plus' may apply to any kind of intelligence, not as a *component* of intelligence, but as an entirely different dimension of thinking and behaviour. It is this approach to creativity that supports the prominent role of creativity in the post-information age we saw in Chapter 1. Not only does IQ-type intelligence seem mediocre in comparison, but many of the IQ aspects of human intelligence are likely soon, along with information handling, to have been delegated to computers.

Domain knowledge

Knowledge is another feature of creativity that is linked with intelligence. According to the '10-year rule', outstanding creative people spend 10 or so years in a particular domain before producing their acclaimed creative product, such as an invention, published paper or artistic or musical creation. Knowledge is equivalent to the 'crystallized intelligence' described by Cattell, and which he compared with 'fluid intelligence', a more creative and adaptive variety. Sternberg and Lubert, however, don't include knowledge as part of intelligence, although it does form part of creativity.

Knowledge is a mega aspect of creativity that you can do something about and so boost your CQ. It is a matter of application and commitment at a conscious level and you don't have to wait for the Muse. It reflects the '99 per cent perspiration' as against '1 per cent inspiration' remark attributed to Thomas Edison of light-bulb fame. As it happens, creativity works the other way round. It doesn't call upon exertion and effort. It feels that way as the inspiration doesn't involve conscious effort. We remember the boring or unpleasant parts when time goes slowly. However, maybe Edison made it hard on himself. After coming up with the filament idea, he could surely have delegated the hundreds of routine trials to a government-subsidized work experience recruit, taken the eventual credit like senior professors do, and put his scarce creativity to inventing a mobile telephone or Walkman. That's being both intelligent and creative, however you define the words. Intelligence comes in many varieties and each has its own relationship to the varieties of creativity we have been discussing.

The perfect partnership

Where does this leave creativity *vis-à-vis* intelligence? The right brain is not a 'component' of the brain in the way that creativity is defined as a component of intelligence. Indeed, the unconscious part of the brain has been likened to the submerged part of an iceberg and is said to account for maybe 99 per cent of all our behaviour (that figures, as we can only handle half a dozen thoughts consciously but have billions to call upon). All our habitual behaviour operates unconsciously, of course, or at least without *attention*. The parallel processing, association-searching right brain seems to be of an altogether higher order both in capacity and quality, and in the complexity of the problems it solves. Insightful solutions can sometimes baffle our conscious logical minds as we work out the logic backwards. It is not surprising that in past centuries creative ideas were thought to come from some outside, omniscient source. That's the way it still feels.

All the seemingly 'clever' functions happen unconsciously, such as:

■ trawling mega memory databases;
■ intuitively redefining problems;

- making 'aha' associations from disparate, remote bits of memory;
- solving intractable problems;
- incubation ('sleeping on a problem') – the epitome of efficiency;
- creating original ideas;
- visualizing new scenarios as the basis for successful behaviour.

These are more associated with the right cortex and mid-brain than the linguistic, logical left brain that we often associate with intelligence of the IQ type. They follow their own strange rules, such as:

- the harder you try the more difficult it gets;
- think about something else and the answer will come;
- if it feels right it probably is;
- you are more productive when showering or driving than when you are at work;
- a well-considered problem might well disappear by the following morning.

We are still guessing about these ways of the mind, and the differences that different modes of thinking produce in different people, as we have seen. But the fundamental difference between linear intelligence and creativity is well founded in our actual neurophysiology. This gives us the underlying confidence we need to release our true creative powers.

Shaping or adapting

Sternberg gave us one of the most universally accepted definitions of intelligence: 'The ability to purposively adapt to, shape and select environments.' R Osche, however, said: 'If intelligence means selecting and shaping environments, it is creativity.'

In order to select or shape the environment, you need the imagination to create a vision of what that environment will be and how the idealized environment can become a reality. You create your own inner, multi-sensory world. That, in essence, is human creativity. Uniquely, we can:

- think about thinking;
- be aware of being aware;
- re-experience and edit the past;
- envisage the future.

Chimpanzees don't bemoan their childhood opportunities or get hung up about the coming weekend. We can change the environment before it changes us.

On the other hand, the ability to adapt to the environment, or to change *oneself* to suit the environment, requires little or no creativity. We do it, but it is one of our many animal rather than human traits. We do something similar at school and in a job – keep our head down, fit in without rocking the boat, being 'different' or changing anything – or risk a low grade or job prospects. Sternberg's 'shaping and selecting environments' is what we do best, and it is a singularly creative feat.

Seen in this light, everything we do requires creative endeavour. Even for the routines we get machines to do, we have to creatively design and make machines first, then keep telling them what to do. This requires different degrees and types of intelligence, depending on the task in hand and the environment. For example, a creative artist might not require much IQ-type intelligence, whereas a Nobel prize-winning physicist certainly would. This turns the tables on intelligence as we have come to use the term. We could argue the converse: that different degrees of creativity are required in different fields of intelligent behaviour. For example, if fish and game are plentiful, the hunter does not require much creativity, whereas when they are scarce and survival depends on thinking success, he must be more creative. Looked at in this way, creativity and intelligence are different, interdependent processes that are 'reconciled' (remember Sperry's experiments in Chapter 3) and controlled at the top 'self' level. This fits well with what we know of separate brains operating as an integrated system, itself part of a larger, holistic, interdependent mind–body system as we saw in Chapter 3. Shaping and being shaped happen at the same time.

Here is the bottom line: both processes are essential for human endeavour, but most of our western education and institutions model the left-brain kind of intelligence, and neutralize or suppress creativity. Those who display greater creativity in a world in which it is so scarce (above the age of five) therefore achieve disproportionately successful outcomes. Fortunately, we can increase our creativity or CQ, just as we can our academic or adaptive aspects of intelligence – it just requires a different approach and know-how. We can have our say both in shaping and also in the way we adapt, or are shaped.

Buy low, sell high: the investment theory

According to Sternberg and Lubart's investment theory, creative people buy low and sell high – in the world of ideas. In other words, they take unpopular or rejected ideas and convince people of their worth. Then they 'sell' them high as ideas upon which others can capitalize. They then conceive other unlikely ideas and do the same with them. It is not that creative people have no interest in the final outcome of their creativity, or that they are immune to normal material ambitions; it is rather that they lose interest at that stage in the process. Their motivation has transferred to something else and demands their full attention.

The investment theory is an example of the variety of intelligence that is a component (subset) of creativity, rather than the other way round, which is more commonly thought. Sternberg and Lubert argued that there are six main elements that make up creativity:

■ knowledge;
■ intelligence;

- ▨ thinking styles;
- ▨ personality;
- ▨ motivation;
- ▨ the environment.

Intelligence is one aspect, and in turn comprises three aspects that form the triarchic theory of intelligence:

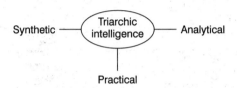

This is known as the triarchic theory. Synthetic ability is the ability to generate novel, high quality ideas that are appropriate to the task in hand. One of the features of synthetic ability is that of redefining problems. This is a common feature of problem solving and creativity. It might result in a problem turning into an opportunity, or being considerably simplified when viewed from another perspective. It may mean going against the crowd, however, and this is where the practical aspect of triarchic intelligence comes in. Creativity applies to everyday situations and practical issues and usually ideas have to be 'sold' to others before they come to fruition. This is akin to interpersonal intelligence in Gardner's multiple intelligences model. It is often a weak link in the chain for many creative people with an introverted personality.

The synthetic aspect of intelligence also applies to so-called 'selective encoding', which involves:

- ▨ selecting relevant from irrelevant information;
- ▨ combining bits of information in novel ways;
- ▨ relating new information to old information in novel ways.

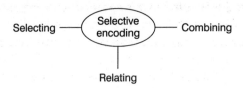

These were considered part of creativity, but outside 'intelligence', and equate to the holistic, associative thinking we have already met. These features have the advantage of being relatively easy to test using mathematical insight problems. For example, 'If you have blue socks and brown socks in a drawer mixed in a ratio of 4 to 5, how many socks do you have to take out of the drawer to be sure of having a pair of each colour?' Interestingly, the researchers in this case found that it was possible to teach elementary school children to improve their insightful thinking – or CQ. That is, their scores, on objectively measurable criteria, increased.

Analysis is akin to more orthodox thinking as in IQ tests. It has creative aspects, however, such as deciding what sort of analysis will prove to be the most illuminating and productive. It seems that we are not lacking in this attribute, although it tends to get overvalued. Hence the derogatory remark 'analysis paralysis' applied to business graduates. Unlike the creative attributes we have discussed, analysis to a degree that leaves human left brains far behind is within the scope of desktop computers. That's a clue to the kind of intelligence we should aspire to.

The intelligence relationship

Intelligence is high on the agenda of psychology, the young science of the mind and its relationship with creativity. More recently, emotional intelligence, or EQ, has widened the old definition, although it still doesn't major on creativity. IQ in particular has had a bad press and is now believed to be based on too narrow a definition of intelligence, yet psychometric instruments have somehow remained as a legitimate measurement tool. One of the many weaknesses levelled against IQ is that it does not measure creativity, or any intuitive aspect of creativity.

The idea of 'multiple intelligences' has also replaced a single, measurable concept of intelligence. In some cases creativity appears as a *component* of intelligence, or one of several intelligences, or is implicit in an intelligence such as musical intelligence. Either way, creativity doesn't fit as neatly as other mental characteristics, and is no easier to define than intelligence.

Some see creativity as a different dimension of human thinking altogether, or at least a different *kind* of intelligence. It certainly operates differently from what we think of as logical thinking, and seems alien to the objectivity of scientific method. Yet the idea of creativity relates easily to what we all know about how we sometimes think – intuitively, from the 'gut', emotionally, with insight, and in ways such that we may even surprise ourselves. We associate creativity, for instance, with highly subjective thought processes that can hardly be described – like musical appreciation, artistic insight or the spark of an idea – let alone understood and analysed.

That makes measurement of creativity, or creativity quotient (CQ), more difficult than EQ, and much more difficult than IQ. But that doesn't mean that we cannot *identify* creativity, and know it when we see it, just as we can spot a person who has 'people skills' or a 'fertile imagination', or who is 'perceptive' or 'intuitive'. Unlike in the case of IQ, in such cases we 'measure' quality, or characteristics, rather than quantity. Multiple, 'right or wrong' questions do not begin to fathom a person's creative potential.

Special cognitive animal

The same measurement dilemma applies to creativity whether we treat it as a component of intelligence, like people skills or 'interpersonal intelligence', or as a special kind of intelligence out there on its own. It is a special kind of cognitive animal and needs its own special manual. Hence the term I use, CQ, or creativity quotient – the *special factor*, quality or attitude that creative people seem to exhibit.

As it happens, the characteristics of creative people have been known for many years and our understanding of them has changed little. In some circles creativity has been valued highly. Creativity training, for example, has been shown to be effective by the largest profit-making corporations. It is also hot property in the education of younger children. However, organizations tend to address specific aspects of creativity as processes rather than making a 'creative person'. That is probably because of the need to fit a system, follow a replicable formula, measure effectiveness and sell the practice in 'bottom line' terms. Nevertheless, it seems that, like any other kind of intelligence, we can nurture and develop creativity – however we define it and whether or not we measure it in numbers like IQ. In other words, we can do it better if we care to acquire the know-how.

8

Systems and the environment

Without an end product of some sort, it is hard to show what is creative, or has creative value. For instance, unless consumers buy a new product, the chances are we would never know about its being created. Likewise, if art critics and the public had not valued Van Gogh's paintings, many years after his penniless death, we would probably not consider them creative, but merely the childish, psychotic indulgences they were thought to be at the time. Even the most objective creativity tests are designed and judged by people, who in turn get their values from the surrounding culture.

Creativity needs an audience. It depends on what other people think about what a person creates. If creativity has any meaning, it must refer to a process that creates a product or idea that is recognized and adopted by others. It operates within a *system*, whether of a few 'judges' in an area of knowledge or domain, an organization, or a wider cultural grouping. We can refer to this larger system broadly as the environment, which includes the wider culture covered in more detail in the next chapter. Within the many definitions of creativity, this environmental feature is common, although excluded from some narrower definitions. The wider cultural environment, such as between east and west, is covered in the next chapter.

The creative environment

This 'systems' view of creativity departs a long way from the more traditional view of creativity as the novel thought process of individuals. The influence of many environmental factors is borne out, however, by longitudinal studies of living people as well as historical records. For example, some potentially very creative people finish up in very ordinary occupations, whilst others who lack early creative attributes produce works of art or inventions that are judged to be highly creative. In one study, young women in art school showed as much potential as male students, yet 20 years later none of the cohort of women had achieved outstanding recognition, whereas several of the cohort of men had.

The simple fact is that good ideas do not automatically turn into accepted creative products. It happens within a wider system of people, traditions and cultures. If you want to be creative, and be *seen* to be creative, or to have whatever you produce accepted by a wider audience, you will have to take your particular environment into account. In some cases you may be able to change your physical environment, such as whether you work on your own or for an employer.

Domains and fields

These outside influences and constraints have always been generally accepted. In creativity research, creativity tests are sometimes judged by 'raters' who decide on the originality and usefulness of responses – such as a story ending or the appropriateness of things you can do with a paper clip. Judges rely, in turn, on their different experience, background, values and personal preferences. They cannot begin to determine objectively what creativity is, yet can influence what is a 'creative product'. But not with impunity; they themselves are part of a 'system' to which they conform, and depend in turn on the wider acceptance of society in the job they do.

Creative ideas will be lost forever unless they are recognized as such and adopted into the domain.

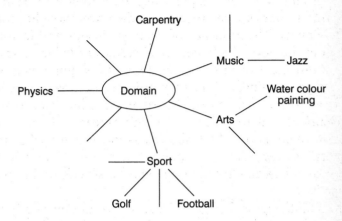

Change will be accepted or rejected by those who in effect control the domain. These are the gatekeepers or jury – the 'field'. In this context the field is not the whole discipline, such as chemistry or woodworking – that is, all chemists and carpenters. Rather, it comprises the relatively few people who *influence* the domain, including its boundaries and any laws or rules to which it subscribes. This will include, for example, teachers, editors, critics, curators, sponsors, professors and suchlike.

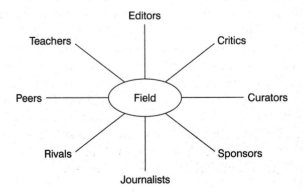

The creative person is therefore part of a bigger ecological system comprising many other people and a cultural, political and religious environment. This view might even suggest that creativity is not the process of an individual, or even that individual's creative 'products', but simply the result of social systems and a culture that makes judgements about persons and products. In other words, a social construct.

P-creativity and H-creativity

Alternatively, like Abraham Maslow, we can define creativity, not as the outcome of a process, but as the process itself. Originality, for instance, can mean originality to the person, rather than to the wider field. In one sense a person is no less creative because somebody thousands of miles away happened to get the same idea sooner. But in a historical sense only the first discovery or invention is original. Otherwise, somebody who comes up with a scientific formula such as Einstein did, without knowing it had already been discovered, would be as creative as Einstein.

These distinctions have been referred to as P-creativity (psychological, or personal) and H-creativity (historical) respectively. They mainly affect the originality aspects of creativity, and especially affect the significance of the 'system'. AI (artificial intelligence) now has computers producing 'original' discoveries such as Euclidian theorems based on the data known at historical times, simulating the way the original insight came. However, the fact that you can get a machine to do something may be an argument against that something being called creative. In any case somebody (a 'system') has to judge between machine and man-made outputs and it comprises people rather than machines.

Personal novelty will not usually stack up as real creativity when we take the environment into account. Taking an insular, personal perspective, few eminent artists and scientists would top the creativity charts, as neither they, nor any of us, can think as creatively as a child who sees everything through fresh eyes.

This approach to creativity is fine if creativity is just an admirable personal trait, but it doesn't mean much in the real world, where creative accomplishment means having something to show for it. The 'useful' or 'appropriate' part of the popular definitions of creativity we met in Chapter 2 gives a clue as to the importance of the context or environment.

Another approach is to treat the personal and environmental, or systemic aspects of creativity separately: 1) the personal creative process; 2) the creativity you need to persuade others of the usefulness of your ideas.

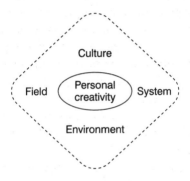

In the first case the creative person and process is everything, whatever emerges. In the second case the environment, or system, is everything. Without such creativity we would never know who had the first kind, let alone make a judgement about it.

The environmental, or 'social acceptance' approach seems unfair, however, on original thinkers who are never recognized. However, it avoids recognizing novelty and originality – often no more than psychotic nonsense or a world of dreams – for their own sake. The great creative geniuses of history are famous because we have made them so, by virtue of the products they gave us, rather than their own creative feelings or assertions. Boxer Mohammed Ali (like racing driver Senna and footballer Pele an example of creativity in sport) declared he was 'the greatest' but knocked a few big people to the floor as evidence to the world that he was. Evaluation is not usually on a grand, historical or global scale, of course. The 'system' in which we operate is a company, school, social circle, professional body and such like. Each has its 'gatekeepers' and 'influencers' who determine values, traditions, standards and meanings such as 'creative'.

Jury and gatekeepers

Although creativity doesn't occur in isolation from its 'system', the 'jury', or the field in which a domain is valued, may be small in number. For instance, not many people were qualified to judge whether Einstein's general theory of relativity was a genuinely creative breakthrough in science. It rested on a small, elite audience who made up that special field of knowledge and acted as 'gatekeepers' to the domain. This select 'field' decided on what could be added to and discarded from the domain and, in particular, defined its boundaries.

To change its boundaries a domain needs what Kuhn terms a paradigm shift. In such cases the rest of us are happy to go along with it. If not, we probably won't have any say within that domain anyway, because we don't possess the necessary knowledge or understand the jargon. Unless, that is, we have got a lot of power and can influence the domain other than through expertise. This applied to the church at the time of Galileo and others who were extending their own scientific domains and stepping on the toes of other domains, including the church itself. Sometimes a creative person has to fight his or her domain corner to be sure his or her creativity is recognized.

Today, a government, sponsor or industrial lobby can influence the course of scientific research and technology and the value of the creative products that emerge. 'System' means any social, political, religious, professional etc system. According to the systems approach an appreciative grandparent may be as influential a part of the system that judges a child's work as a music or art teacher.

The 'systems' approach, although not as dominant as the personal 'trait' or 'process' approaches, is more obvious in cases of 'real' art, or in areas that we culturally deem to be creative, or 'arty'. Take the audience for modern art. The 'jury' or 'field', whether in Paris, London or New York, is probably not much bigger than Einstein's field, and the same applies to fashion and gourmet food. In each of these cases, the 'jury' when it comes to creativity are the buyers, consumers, critics, peers and public who form the guardians of the domain (such as in this case modern art). These in turn interact within a wider culture, or larger 'system'. The jury decides on who and what is creative. As gatekeepers they protect the 'integrity' of the domain. Any old Einstein cannot gatecrash.

What is 'creative', which we can hardly define anyway, changes as these different environments value the new over the old and accept or reject change. At the extreme, creativity can depend on the whim of an individual sponsor, critic, media tycoon or popular guru. Outside a system, creativity may be no more than a fertile imagination. That's fine if it is what you want of your creativity, but most people need some recognition and to create something of value to others than themselves. So you may wish to decide who you want to be recognized by for your creativity. This may influence your creative 'products' and your whole approach to being creative.

Influencers

The systemic environment adds other influences. For example:

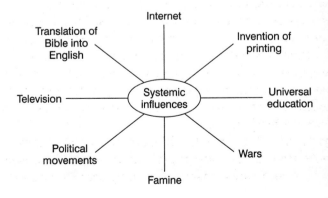

These – which are just the more obvious ones – all upset comfortable fields of knowledge, and proliferated the field. The Nazi movement in the 1930s is an example of the influence of a political movement, and the war that followed of the way people's world view can change. Language barriers such as Latin and Greek protected professions such as the church, law and medicine, and these were in time broken down and democratized. At the same time new domains arose – and continue to do so today at a faster pace – along with the advance of science and technology. Influences like television, although outside the domain of expertise (such as sport, art or music), get to say who is a good leader, the best footballer, jazz pianist and so on – or who is creative. Even individuals, in a consumer society, can make a mark, like members of the domain jury.

We can only define creativity in terms of its domain, such as modern art, bookkeeping or molecular science, and the culture or environment in which that domain exists. So the idea of a creativity measure, or quotient, is at best a moveable feast. But that is fine for most of us – we live with the changing system unless we know enough to influence it. You may not want to become creative if you are the only person who thinks you are. Even Van Gogh sought recognition. He didn't get it because his contemporary audience didn't value what he did – the *system* decided. And for every Van Gogh whose true creativity was eventually recognized by succeeding cultures, there are probably countless artists and inventors we have never heard of, so their work is not even judged. Were they creative? We cannot begin to answer because we don't know who they were and what they produced. The *system* and its influencers determined their success, and the same applies to us today.

Conformity and creativity

Hence the need for a more objective definition of creativity, including 'creative product'. It needs to consist of more than subjective originality, such as would apply to bizarre, psychotic ravings and childish babble. Paradoxically, the greatest works of art – however creative – tend to *conform* to the traditions of their domain. They are measured within a wider system or environment and tend to reflect it. Artists and musicians typically followed a particular school or style, borrowing unashamedly from the current popular masters. Only rarely was a boundary removed by a new movement such as impressionism, or the abandonment of signature keys in musical composition. Einstein similarly moved the boundaries – or rewrote the rule book – in his theory of time and space. He changed the system. However, that was one achievement. In other respects he conformed to his domain, culture and generation as we all do.

Such paradigm changes are the exception rather than the rule. Individual creativity usually conforms to environmental influences even though it doesn't like them. Youthful devotees of popular music and fashion culture are more likely to be followers than leaders; they may be 'way out', but conform rigidly to a sub-culture or 'domain'. The effect of the system is all-embracing and can be insidious, however, and creative people will tend to deny their conformity.

According to the systems model creativity involves individuals, domains and fields:

The domain is the existing cultural pattern, without which creativity cannot be measured – 'new' has to be viewed in relation to 'old'. As we saw earlier, creativity does not exist in a vacuum. The domain might be carpentry, radiology, country and western music, painting and decorating, or whatever. Without established traditions and norms, as all domains have, individual carpenters and radiologists cannot be measured in terms of originality or creativity – in other words, in what is *new to the domain*. That is for the domain jury and gatekeepers – the system – to decide.

The systems context clearly reduces the possibility of individual creativity being given free rein, or even recognized. Historically, a person's own position or influence within a domain – regardless of innate personal creativity – has had a major influence on creative recognition. Until quite recently, most scientific advances were made by men who had the means and leisure to indulge their interests, such as clergymen, successful physicians and 'gentlemen' of independent means. Like Leonardo da Vinci, they were 'all-rounders' with the world's knowledge in their library at home. They could exercise *influence* in their own right, regardless of their creative contribution. And even these reflected a contemporary culture of systematic observation of nature and keeping records, upon which the eventual creative products of these privileged gentlemen depended. That doesn't mean they didn't have individual creative traits, but rather that, as the above model shows, it was only one of three main factors. Paradoxically, conformity may help a person to gain recognition within a system, whether a domain of expertise, an organization or a social grouping.

Creating paradigms

To gain acceptance within a field, creativity has to be more than just a blip of a change. At the extreme it involves a fundamental change in a symbolic system such that it is bound to affect the thoughts and opinions of the field, and the boundaries of the domain – a paradigm change in Kuhn's terminology. Or a 'meme', or building block of culture, in the terminology of Dawkin.

Memes

A meme is like a gene in that it carries instructions for action. For example, a cake recipe tells us what ingredients to mix, musical notation tells us what notes to play and how long they last, and so on. So to make a creative impact on a domain, you would not just have to compose a great new song or piece of music, but pioneer or personally influence a whole musical tradition such as jazz, blues or rock and roll. Or as an artist, pioneer cubism, impressionism or a significant artistic movement. The chances are that if you produced a string of great songs, or scores of great paintings, you would make an impact on your field anyway, and bring about change by ratcheting the domain to a higher cultural or aesthetic level. Either way, creativity would be more than a one-off product, and certainly more than an invisible, internal creative process or trait. Creativity would depend on acceptance within your field, and perhaps also your influence as a person as well as an artist. This would mean more than originality alone. The creative 'product' would have to bring real and lasting change to the domain. This is not run-of-the-mill creativity, but potentially we can all make such an impact on our own system, or world of influence.

Creative ambition

The systemic approach to creativity also applies to the individual who has no ambitions of making paradigm advances or gaining special recognition. In this case, the principle that creativity doesn't happen in a vacuum still applies. The 'system' in this case is the hierarchy of goals and desires of the individual. The creative product will be:

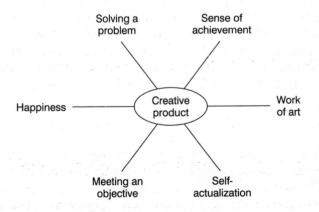

or whatever. In other words, it will be for a reason, or *purpose*. Thus the 'usefulness' criterion does not have to be met in terms of the wider society, but in terms of the individual's own life and intentions. The 'field' is then the company you work for, your family, or the circle of friends whose respect you value, as the case may be – any part of a system upon which your values are based and your personal goals depend. Happiness, a common goal, for example, usually involves others than yourself within the system. Like creativity, it does not happen in isolation. If one of your intentions is to gain wider recognition, such as in your trade or profession or in a sports league, then the wider system will come into play anyway, and determine the success or failure of your creative product. Either way, creativity only happens as part of a system.

As an individual, you can maximize your personal creativity by focusing on an important goal rather than a secondary one – something high up your hierarchy of goals. We have already touched on the importance of motivation, and the way in which highly creative people become absorbed in the task in hand. This means that the choice of task or area of interest is critical, as it has to carry your motivation through to the end product. Thus what is most important in your life – what motivates (provides a motive, or literally moves) you – is the best candidate in which to exercise creativity. (Motivation is covered in more depth in Chapter 10.) For this reason, many people show creativity in personal hobbies and after-work interests rather than in their full-time job, to the enormous loss of employers. Having chosen your project, rather than having it allocated by a boss, organization or authority figure, you are more likely to display your creative powers and succeed in what you do. The 'system' is whoever you display your creative powers to, and whoever may influence your definition of 'success'.

9

Culture and creativity

Creativity isn't a personal island. It depends on the environment, culture and in particular the peers who decide on what is and what is not creative. It goes without saying that the 'parent' culture can have either an enhancing or a detrimental effect on a person's creativity. It may allow and encourage freedom of expression on the one hand or impose constraints on individuality on the other. Other people may have a different opinion about what is creative than the person setting out to create. Or the domain may support and 'sell' a creative product to the wider world. It follows that if we can operate in a more conducive environment we will increase our potential creativity as individuals and organizations. We have looked at the various systems in which creativity operates. In this chapter we will consider more specifically the influence of the 'parent' or macro culture.

As well as understanding the culture in which we exercise our creativity, we can gain a lot by understanding other cultures and seeing things from different perspectives. Creativity techniques attempt to stimulate different perspectives such as in 'reversal' (Chapter 14) but cultural awareness is a less contrived way to foster CQ. We don't just learn from different approaches to a task or problem, but we encounter different creative products and world views. These churn up our thinking patterns at deeper and wider levels. That fuels true creativity, so cultural exposure is to be welcomed.

Several personal aspects of creativity are usually treated as main variables – typically:

■ intelligence;
■ knowledge;
■ cognitive style;
■ personality;
■ motivation.

Culture and environment are missing from this popular list. The surrounding 'environment' usually covers the physical setting, the family, school or workplace, the field of endeavour and the culture.

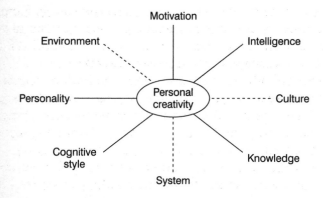

The term 'culture' may also apply to an organization as well as a larger national or religious social grouping. We will focus mainly on the wider culture, such as in the common distinction between western and eastern, but you will find that much applies equally to smaller cultural units such as a small business.

Cultural systems

Culture refers to the shared behaviours, rules, values and symbols of a grouping of people. It governs the way they interact with their environment and the people they relate to. This does not involve the internal workings of creativity – the Muse or some mystical, innate source of inspiration. We are not born with a culture gene but the influence of culture can seem just as genetic as the big nose on your father's side. We learn our 'parent' culture from the earliest age and it is passed on from generation to generation, but it finishes up as neural circuits like any other trait, genetic or otherwise. The culture may have geographical, racial, religious, political and other such boundaries, comprising common interests, loyalties, origins and suchlike.

Culture changes over time, as do values at the individual level, so its effect on creativity will also change. However, culture at a national or religious, as compared with, say, at an organization level, doesn't change too quickly – at least when compared with technology and other social changes. In fact, the human tendency is to inertia rather than change. The overall effect on creativity of a culture can therefore be identified fairly reliably from the snapshots that researchers take.

The ideas of both creativity and culture go back millennia, of course. Here, we are concerned with the relatively recent period during which creativity has been researched in a scientific or quasi-scientific way. In addition, we are concerned with how culture affects our own personal creativity.

You may find ideas from other cultures generally more appealing and stimulating. On the other hand, you may feel that foreign ideas are disturbing and unhelpful. But the quest for personal creativity doesn't stop at familiar boundaries, nor can we close our eyes and ears to whatever is out there. Creativity involves introspection and honesty, and an open mind even to ideas that seem crazy. Each culture – or each person – sees the other in just such a way. Creativity, like dreams and young children, gets as close as you get to stark honesty.

Western definitions of creativity

Creativity is usually defined as producing what is both novel and useful. This is a western definition, however. The definitions of creativity, as well as its products and the attitude towards it, vary from culture to culture and this immediately reveals some major differences. Further cultural differences appear as we consider aspects of creativity such as different processes and products and the traits of creative people.

It may help to first illustrate how the definitions of creativity we have used in this book mainly reflect a typical western, as compared with eastern culture. We see the 'western' definition reflected in popular creativity tests, such as the *Torrance Test of Creative Thinking*. Tasks are scored on fluidity (number of ideas), flexibility (the variety of ideas) and originality (the statistical rarity of ideas). These tend to reflect a western 'world view'. For example, western culture generally:

■ encourages individual achievement rather than collective endeavour;
■ encourages productivity and variety, as can be seen in any supermarket or electronic gadget retailer;
■ promotes the work ethic;
■ supports individual liberty and independence and the right to be different;
■ promotes building for the future and material progress.

Thus cultural attitudes towards creativity are reflected in the main *values* a social group espouses, such as freedom, individuality and material progress. Originality, fluidity and flexibility fuel these western cultural views. New products, processes and discoveries make life better and promise more for our children. They also support competitiveness, another major feature of material advancement and capitalist politics.

Likewise, 'western creativity' is compatible with scientific research and the paradigm breakthrough advances we associate with well-known historical figures. The creative ideas that produce a constant supply of new products figure large in any research into creativity. This also reflects the importance in the west of material products, innovation, and visible evidence of success. From time to time creativity goes out of fashion, at least in its narrower definition, but generally it is a positive phenomenon and in recent years has been increasingly so.

Eastern definitions of creativity

The eastern idea of creativity is more to do with:

- a *state* of personal fulfilment;
- a *connection* to a tradition or earlier time in their history (including primordial);
- the *expression* of an inner sense of ultimate reality.

It is linked usually to different forms of meditation, as this is the way we see into our inner selves, where creativity happens. It is closer to Maslow's more limited 'top of the needs ladder' concept of self-actualization, or personal fulfilment, in western psychology. The eastern process of creativity seeks to find unconscious truths that are *already there*, rather than create something new. It therefore seeks to *re-create*, or reactivate, rather than create.

In some eastern countries creativity is much more a religious expression than a secular problem-solving process. In western culture we tend to use creativity to solve problems, create opportunities and generally achieve material progress. The religious view of time and history as cyclical tends not to value originality as in the west, whereas this is a common feature of some eastern religions. For example, creativity may imitate the supreme or spiritual, and thus, by definition, stay within certain ageless boundaries, or maintain a traditional world view. With a non-cyclical view, the future is unknown and open to discovery and novelty as in the Judaeo-Christian west. In the east generally, creativity, although present, may be more to do with reinterpreting *existing* knowledge and wisdom rather than producing the paradigm advances extending a domain, so valued in the west.

Creativity in the western sense of originality and flexibility may be exercised in some parts of an eastern culture but not others, so across the board comparisons are difficult. For example, variations in depicting a certain deity artistically may be restricted, whereas this may not apply to lesser deities (such as household, or personal gods) and to the depiction of other beings that have their own religious significance. In such less-constrained cases, which are too numerous to categorize, creativity in, say, art and music may closely mirror the western definition.

Comparing cultures

Although its connotations are limited to certain stereotypes, as we have seen, western culture is positive about creativity – it's 'a good thing'. We observe this in the trend to incorporate it into schools and also in major companies as a strategy and training topic. We also have high regard for historical figures (especially western ones), such as Einstein and Edison, who are considered to be very creative. Although not so extensive, similar positive views are found in non-western cultures. For example, creative architectural geniuses among the West African Hausa are admired and emulated by builders. Similarly, there are various deities that are believed to influence creativity through dreams and inspiration. But these individual instances are specific and do not always represent the cultural world view. In general, creativity is more widely adopted in artistic, poetic and everyday life, where people have freedom to draw upon their own experience without religious or traditional constraints.

It may be interesting to note that the origin of creativity as a cultural construct seems to date to the many kinds of creation myths, so it is an old, deep-seated idea. This includes concepts of the creator as craftsman (such as potter, weaver or blacksmith) so there is a 'handiwork' or *artistic execution* element. This world genesis connection, whatever form it takes, seems to be universal and perhaps adds to the mystery that surrounds creativity.

Cultural processes

Cultural differences are also found in the process of creativity. The western process typically comprises preparation, incubation, illumination and verification, as described in Chapter 5.

There is far less evidence of a common process in non-western cultures. However, a study of 155 traditional painters in India provides some interesting analogies. A four-stage process is also described:

1. contact with the subjective region of the artist's mind, involving symbolic and religious rituals such as the burning of incense;
2. internal identification with the subject matter of the painting;
3. illumination;
4. the social communication of the personal realizations.

The illumination stage is similar to the western example. However, this seems to be in the nature of personal enlightenment in Chapter 5 rather than related to the subject matter, such as the work of art or the problem to be solved in a western creative context.

The final stage is roughly equivalent to the western 'verification' stage. It suggests a wide definition and special significance of creativity. However, the emphasis is on sharing, or passing on enlightenment rather than exposing personal creativity to outside evaluation. None the less, the process itself and its importance to the artists is a cultural phenomenon, like yoga, martial arts and traditional dance. Thus evaluation by the culture is implicit.

As we have seen, meditation is a common aspect of the creative process. The main difference from the western creative process is emphasis on the personal, emotional, psychic and sometimes religious aspects. We have witnessed much crossing of cultural borders, especially since the personal liberation and self-expression of the 1960s. This seems to have been in an east to west direction, such as in the interest in yoga, meditation and various martial arts. However, a less overt, and possibly greater cross-cultural influence in the other direction has come from television, cinema and western popular culture.

These major cultural differences affect the definition of creativity, the description of a creative person, and the value placed on creative products. It raises important doubts about the validity of western-designed psychometric tests, such as Torrance's. It does help to show, however, that creativity only makes sense in the context of a person, their goals and values, and the cultural traditions they adhere to.

Notwithstanding the broader definition, we can all be creative, and can all gain benefits, including tangible benefits if we so direct our creativity. Cultural awareness can bring choice rather than restriction, just as does exposure to new experiences and ideas nearer home. We are also free to consider the cultural constraints we conform to. Creative people are known to be independently minded, and not enamoured of authority, even of a native, ambient culture. This is more apparent in their employment (and self-employment) status but reaches to political and religious levels also. You can decide whether these extrinsic motivators help or hinder your desire to be creative, and the more personal intentions to which you wish to direct it.

Sacred and secular

Culture can have either a positive or negative effect on personal creativity. Arab students who showed plenty of creative fluidity in answering standard psychometric questions were very limited in their replies to a question asking what would happen if places of worship ceased to exist – some refused to answer the question. Most people have a few creative blind spots resulting from cultural and religious influences. These need not be a problem if you identify and *choose* them. But, as with any belief system, when they operate unconsciously they can scupper your more conscious intentions and produce unaccounted behaviour. Inner conflict is best resolved by reconciling the conflicting 'parts' – the different right- and left-brain, holistic–detail processes we met in Chapter 3.

In some cultures creativity is encouraged in carving secular objects but not in religious representations. For example, a fundamental motif is not open to change, but sub-themes are. The head, face and hands of a being may be immutable, but what they have in their hands is open to creativity. Likewise, there may be no such restriction on landscape paintings, in which creativity can flourish. In another case, the shape of pottery may be fixed by tradition, but its decoration wide open to individual creativity.

In most cultures, some aspects of popular art will reflect true creativity, which may be more or less encouraged. Generally, the more a culture seeks to protect and maintain traditions, the less creativity is to be expected in those areas, and the less material progress when measured in gross national product. However, even within cultural boundaries, a person can usually exercise more choice than at first sight. It just means identifying the part a cultural system plays in your life and deciding what you really want.

Selecting creativity

The 'selectivity' of creativity in different cultures occurs widely, and Samoan dance has been used as an example. Three kinds of dance (women's, men's and comedians') are strictly adhered to in their steps, order and positions – the choreographical structure. However, within this basic framework the dancers are expected to create their own style, so change is gradually adopted at a surface level. Change to the dance *structure* is precluded, and this would be equivalent to a scientific paradigm advance in which the domain itself is extended. So clearly, in this case, the fundamental creativity we associate with genius and scientific and artistic breakthroughs will not happen. Traditions are maintained, but at a price to creativity.

Insofar as such cultural constraints affect education, art, commerce and politics, they will limit innovation and affect economic performance as well as artistic development. If economic achievement is not the goal, then such a world view may not be to any detriment. The detriment, however, is across the cultural board and we cannot always measure the price of restricting creative thought. Historically, freedom of thought has been linked to no less than the advance of civilization. A distinction also needs to be made between personal pleasure and enlightenment (say through meditation) and creative products as we discussed in Chapter 6, which may well have a ripple effect on the cultural and economic environment – or on *human progress*.

In many cases there will be conflict between maintaining cultural traditions and the economic demands of modern life in the shrinking global village. The Internet and television, for example, tend to break down cultural as well as geographical boundaries. Once having recognized this, the individual is free to evaluate the importance of their cultural ties and optimize their personal creativity within these bounds. This may well mean being selective in the kind of creative products you aspire to. Understanding other cultures will itself add new world views – as choices or resources – that will extend a person's mental territory, and enrich their creativity.

The selectivity of the influence of culture on creativity can be seen in music as well as other forms of art. One tribal culture maintains that 'there is only one way to sing a (particular) song'. If a religious song is sung to an incorrect tune, ritual weeping follows. In one Far-Eastern culture, innovation in music is a group endeavour. Different groups are expected to differ in style, but individual musicians are expected to be stereotyped and to blend in with the music anonymously. This probably reflects the wider cultural predominance of the collective voice of the society as compared with individual expression. In other words, it is not just a feature of music or other practices we usually associate with creativity, but a more fundamental cultural view.

Gender and culture

In a similar way, in some cultures there is a gender difference, which reflects itself in artistic expression. In one case, both men and women can be creative, but this is restricted to particular musical genres. In this case songs that express the personal emotions of the singer are acceptable for women, and songs that provoke a collective emotional response, such as weeping, are for the men. Gender differences in western culture are more overt and become apparent when creative products are emphasized, such as works of art, registered patents and published academic papers in which males tip the balance (but women had no say in the 'products').

This cultural pick and mix of creativity occurs in every area we typically associate with creativity. Creativity in bead weaving, storytelling, healing ceremonies, or pottery, for instance, may be restricted to just men or women, or open to both. A strong gender difference has been identified in historiometric studies in which few women figure, because of the cultural barriers against them entering or influencing a particular domain. Historically, this gender imbalance applies also to western culture but to a lesser degree in more recent times, perhaps because there are fewer religious and educational restrictions.

Wide differences occur across cultures depending on the kind of creativity measured. For instance, when the *Torrance Test of Creative Thinking* is taken by children and adults around the world, different elements are seen to score differently as between men and women, yet for other elements of the test there are no significant differences. Ignoring the weakness of the psychometric instruments themselves (see Chapter 11), each of these differences is likely to have a cultural explanation. It tells us that, owing to cultural conformity, many people are limiting or quashing their innate creativity. They – and probably in the long run the cultures from which they hail – thus lose out.

Information is valuable and knowledge brings with it choice, such as whether to conform or not to conform to a system. Usually we passively acquiesce to all kinds of 'systemic' and cultural influences without realizing it. But our cultural heritage is rich and potentially a *source* of creativity. Becoming more creative may mean becoming more aware of these influences and consciously opting for creative freedom.

10

The creative power of self-motivation

Highly creative people get absorbed intensely in their work, sometimes foregoing sleep and other necessities of life in their dedicated pursuit of what they want. Historically, creativity and genius have been associated with madness and eccentricity. In any event, we are certain that creativity is associated with high commitment and motivation. This is one of the key factors that account for a person producing creative products, and being known as a 'creative person'. In other words, motivation is not just needed to get a task done (most people are motivated to do certain tasks at certain times), but it is a long-term, quite specific personality trait found in creative people, almost regardless of the task they put their hand to.

Creative people themselves express what motivates them in different ways. The novelist John Irving, who would work 12 hours a day on a book for days on end, said: 'The unspoken factor is love. The reason I work so hard at my writing is that it's not work for me.'

Others speak of the challenge, the magnetic pull of discovering something new, the intellectual 'flow' and almost an addiction to expanding the frontiers of their understanding. These are not the usual external, material motivators we associate with goal achievement and business management. In fact, research has shown that external factors such as monetary rewards may actually reduce a person's creative output.

What is in no doubt is that motivation is an important aspect of creativity – perhaps the single overriding factor. Creative people themselves often deny having special gifts and mental ability, but are usually aware of their high level of motivation. This, they say, accounts for the dedication and sheer hard work that invariably accompanies their creativity. They enjoy what they do – or at least the creative things.

Intrinsic and extrinsic motivation

Some psychologists have postulated that creativity fulfils an unconscious desire 'to atone for aggressive or destructive impulses or to utilize regressive, amoral urges'. Maybe. Others maintain that it takes the role that play serves in children, allowing us to 'work though conflict and imbue a fantasy world with emotional content'. More positively, creativity has been associated with:

- the healthy desire to master one's own environment;
- fulfilling higher-order actualization-type needs such as self-understanding;
- achieving personal order and control;
- the sheer enjoyment and satisfaction from engaging in the creative activity.

The theory that seems to have gained greatest acceptance is that creativity is motivated by the creative task itself. Essentially, there is intrinsic pleasure in the task or project *for its own sake*. A corollary is the proposition that creativity may be inhibited by external motives that somehow detract from the person's enjoyment of the activity.

If such motivation is indeed a critical part of creativity, the question arises as to where this intrinsic motivation comes from. Other people will invariably be engaged on the same sort of projects, or potentially creative activities, yet without the degree of enthusiasm and creative outcomes. This is the proverbial chicken and egg dilemma, or the equivalent of the child's philosophical question 'but who made God?' What induces a person to embark on a task in the first place?

Most people know what it is to be completely absorbed for a prolonged period of time in some interest or hobby and to have enjoyed the flow of creativity *on occasions*. The *process* is common to human beings, and not confined to geniuses. If we can understand the nature of a person's motivation, high creativity might be explained as a matter of the *degree* and *frequency* of whatever is the special motivating force. In both cases the objective, in CQ terms, is to increase *both* rather than one at the expense of the other.

Research dating back many years has identified the relationship between creativity and other personal traits:

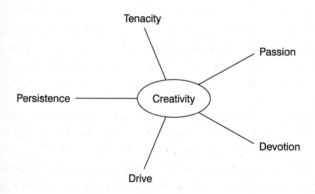

Traits and circumstances

In a few cases there are suggestions as to what processes or circumstances might have produced these laudable traits that contribute to motivation. For example:

■ Creativity only occurs in the absence of external regulation.

▓ Creativity is motivated by a person's desire for self-actualization – a drive which we all have. Maslow defined this as the spontaneous expression of the person whose more basic needs have been satisfied (in fact, few historical examples of creative genius had to concentrate on earning their next meal).

▓ Creativity occurs in a context of self-motivation and self-evaluation, rather than being driven by outside evaluation and rewards.

▓ Freedom from control.

▓ Freedom to exercise unconscious, playful forms of thought.

▓ The exercise of creative powers should form its own, and the most important, reward.

▓ Deep involvement in and commitment to the task in hand.

▓ Creative people generally prefer to work alone.

It seems to boil down to intrinsic rather than extrinsic, ego-involved motivation. In other words, *self-motivation*, but without the need to use willpower and conscious effort. The intrinsic value is in doing the job well and attaining the creative solution.

In the case of extrinsic motivation, the achievement of a creative solution is more likely *a means to some other end*, rather than the end in itself. For example, sometimes extrinsic factors will help to get a person interested in a task, but thereafter creativity will depend on whether they become intrinsically involved. Following the creative period in the task or project, extrinsic motivation may again have a role to play in the equivalent of the final evaluation and execution stages of the job. For example, employees may want to see their ideas brought to fruition in the form of an actual product, have it accepted by their seniors, or adopted into the organization.

Based on the research, external rewards are unlikely to produce more creativity. By the time the creative period is over, the person has probably milked the task for its creative chal-lenge. They will then respond to extrinsic rewards and recogni-tion like anybody else. For example, 'ordinary', extrinsic rewards may motivate the person to attend to less stimulating detail and tie up the loose ends. What we associate with left-brain thinking is at work at these stages in the overall creativity process, and such activities are quite amenable to either a stick or a carrot approach.

Motivators

Intrinsic and extrinsic motivation are factors included in the *Work Preference Inventory* (WPI) and creativity research has been done over the years using this popular psychometric measure. Research typically focuses on the different characteris-tics associated with intrinsic and extrinsic motivation respec-tively. For example:

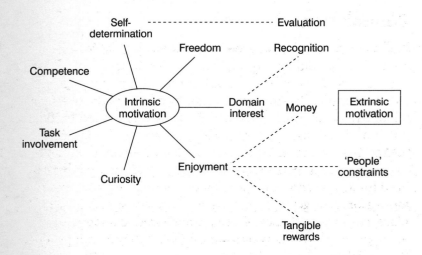

People who score high on the intrinsic scale consistently produce work rated to be more highly creative than those scoring high on extrinsic factors. Similarly, people in profes-sions we usually identify with creativity (artists, research scientists, and such) tend to score high on intrinsic motivation characteristics. This information helps in two main ways: 1) it helps us to understand what creativity is, and in particular where motivation fits in; 2) by developing these attributes you can add practically to your own, overall creativity.

Developing motivating attributes

Some creative attributes seem linked to a person's motivation, although cause and effect may not be clear. We can develop these attributes in different ways, and in general by conscious exploration of new fields of knowledge and skills. Knowledge itself can be motivating. In other cases it may be the challenge of a task and the uncertainty that surrounds it. Developing creative attributes is a sure way of increasing your creativity. CQ is not immutable like your height or the colour of your eyes.

Commitment

High motivation shows itself in the intensity of dedication and long-term commitment to a task or project. Most people experience the odd burst of creativity, but do not have much in their lives as evidence. Intrinsic motivation comes from the task itself, whatever the external outcome or rewards. Attention to external considerations, whether positive or negative, good or bad, means less attention to the job in hand. Greatest creativity happens when a person is intrinsically motivated without the need for any incentive, persuasion or reward. Ordinary external motivators may get us to embark on a project or task in the first place, such as the chance of being transferred to another department and work we enjoy or promotion, but they do not produce the creativity.

The longer and more deeply a person is involved in a domain, or field of interest, the more the subject of interest will absorb their thinking time and energy. This depth of focus and commitment will in turn generate new lines of interest and intellectual challenges – the stuff of creativity. However, time is not the key factor, and we know that many people spend several years in a chosen area of work with little creative output at the end. Even highly creative people will have to apply themselves over a period to make an impact on a complex matter, or a whole domain. If vivid mental imagery comes naturally, as it tends to do with a creative person, then the person will be more likely to get deeply involved in a domain, drawn by the attractive, realistic imagery. Some studies have shown that students who score high on intrinsic imagery (in the *Thematic Apperception Test* [TAT]) persist in a subject longer after leaving school and go on to achieve greater success. Creative people are usually adept at visualization and may use it as a self-motivation skill.

There is still the question, however, of which comes first: the long-term application to the task that tends towards creativity or the internal motivation to get started in the first place and then to keep at it. But even if self-motivation is a 'natural' creative characteristic you can still have it within your control, as you can learn and improve visualization and other intrapersonal intelligence skills that affect your state and foster creativity.

Love

Motivation seems to arise from a simple interest in and love for the job in hand. A major long-term study showed that people who were doing what they loved were more creative in their pursuits. This love or interest may already exist, or it may be stimulated by exposure to the task, and especially any challenging or unusual aspects it promises. Either way, it means you can take creativity into your own hands through the day-to-day experiences you open your life to and the choices you make. The prime factor is a deep love for what you are doing, and that can grow as you open your mind to new experiences. However this intrinsic pleasure comes about, when it does, you will operate in a state of higher than usual creativity.

Most people can identify with such a state of mind even though it doesn't happen very often. It can happen cursorily during a simple task, or it may be a prolonged period of flow, as we discussed in Chapter 5. The attention, pleasure, intensity, minimal effort, and creative products are the common factors.

'Love' for the task may be a compelling interest that can engender love–hate feelings. It engages the emotions as well as the intellect, which explains the degree of commitment and enthusiasm. It invariably involves challenge, risk and uncertainty, and maybe frustration, blind alleys and lean times along the way. Nevertheless, the creative person finds even the most complex problems exciting and seems drawn to extending their personal boundaries of knowledge and skills.

The fact that 'intrinsic' motivation comes from inside doesn't mean that you possess it as a personality trait or that it is a special gift that you've either got or you haven't. On the contrary. By consciously *thinking* about a task or project you can generate motivation, just as the more you think about a dream holiday the more you are motivated towards it, and the more likely it is to happen. In other words, it is in large measure within your control.

Nonconformity

Extrinsic motivation involves the person's ego. Most people will not have the degree of detachment necessary to set aside conventional ideas and the need for recognition in favour of a more risky, unpredictable course. This implies a basic antipathy between conformity and creative thought – a factor that repeats itself in various kinds of creativity research. In particular, people who tend to follow the crowd (or group, as in a 'good team player') will be less likely to get creative ideas than a person who is happy to go it alone, without popular support or acclaim. People who tend to follow a consensus, group view tend to show lower levels of creativity. Being 'accepted' by friends and colleagues can be a major extrinsic motivator but it can have a negative effect on creativity. This is an example of where a personality trait may affect creative output and needs to be taken into account.

Flashes and flow

Creativity based on a person's motivation is not to be confused with the spontaneous eureka sort of creative flash or insight. As we saw earlier, that is part of the four-stage creativity process that includes also periods of time in preparation and evaluation – in other words, more conscious, rational rather than intuitive thought. Motivation will need to sustain the person through the whole creative process, and involves creative production – producing something of value.

When we look at cases of highly creative people it turns out that periods of creativity can be long, spanning maybe years. This matches the historiometric findings that typically a person was completely immersed in their domain before producing real creative products (a period of about 10 years has been widely observed). This helps to explain why such an intense love for the work is required – anything less would hardly sustain such a long period of commitment. It also helps to explain how the creative person can go on to change the domain itself, through a paradigm change of the rules and boundaries. Again, a shorter-term, less intensive commitment would hardly produce the level of knowledge required, for which – to a creative, exploring mind – a single lifetime seems all too short.

Time is needed to acquire skills as well as knowledge, as in the case of a leading musician or painter. It also applies, however, to a scientist who needs to learn the experimental methods to make his or her discoveries and prove his or her theories.

The idea of intrinsic and extrinsic motivation advanced creativity theory to a three-part model that included:

Studies showed that not only do extrinsic rewards not contribute to creativity, but they may actually be detrimental. The idea of rewards is so entrenched in psychology that this was an extraordinary finding, and confirmed the unique role of human creativity. This does not reflect an abnormal disregard for rewards and incentives. It does reflect the person's state of mind and the degree of attention given to the task alone, and necessary for creative outcomes.

Evaluation and inhibition

A lot of the research on motivation concerns the evaluation of creative work or products, and whether expecting one's work to be evaluated affects creativity. For example, in a case we referred to earlier, college women were asked to make a paper collage, in one case with the expectation of evaluation and in another case without. In the first case they were told that their finished designs would be rated by graduate art students. Those in the second group were told that the experimenter was only interested in their *mood* while carrying out the task and the finished designs were not of interest. Artist-judges then ranked the results on creativity (although subjective, this usually gets a high level of agreement between judges). Those who expected their finished work to be evaluated were found to be significantly less creative than the other group. Their creative skills were not in question, but they were not motivated to create with these conditions.

Simple awareness of *possible* evaluation prior to a task has been found to reduce creativity in the ensuing task. Likewise, people are less creative simply by virtue of being watched – something most of us would have intuitively known anyway. Attention is essential for creative output, and this can be diverted to an audience just as it can be to a future reward. This particularly applies to experiments with people with known creative personalities who seem to be more sensitive. To allow for this they tend to distance themselves psychologically from others and so minimize the negative effects of the distraction. It seems as though this important characteristic is more the need for personal detachment from outside influences generally rather than simply the effect of a reward or an explicit accolade such as a high rating or praise. The negative effect on attention outweighs the normal positive effect of a reward.

This matches the personality criteria of enjoying isolation, autonomy and self-reliance. When autonomy is reduced, so is creativity. For example, when children doing a painting were told they must be neat (because it is a rule), their creativity fell. However, when the children were told they should be neat 'so as to keep the materials tidy for the other children', their creativity was not affected. The *perception* of outside authority, rules, constraints and interruptions – as well as evaluation and rewards – dampens the creative spirit or motivation to give the task 100 per cent.

Information and rewards

There is a fine line between perceptions of outside interference or rules, and information intended to help or simply inform but that might be construed as interference. Thus, when subjects treat what they are told as *useful information* – say to improve their skill and help them to be more productive or original – it does not have the same detrimental effect. Indeed the tone or manner in which the instruction is given is sufficient to have an effect on this highly sensitive characteristic of creativity. Although we only have anecdotal evidence, this may well explain the fact that many people do not exercise the same level of creativity at work as in their hobbies and at the weekend. A request from a boss, and even the hierarchical environment itself, may be enough to demotivate a person in the sensitive area of creativity.

Extrinsic rewards

Straightforward rewards, even of high value, may *reduce* creativity. This applies even when it is known that creativity, rather than the utility of the end product, is the criterion for success. This doesn't mean that the people are not attracted to material rewards. Such rewards have the expected positive effect when linked to measures other than creativity, such as persistence, accuracy, or working extra hours for an employer. It is as though the person knows that they cannot summon up originality and fluidity, whatever the incentive, just as we cannot recall a forgotten name as long as we consciously focus on remembering it. People known for their creativity are intuitively aware of this and may actually set out to avoid conditions where they cannot mentally freewheel, without interference.

Even when the reward is given *before* the task (as a 'please' rather than 'thank you'), the same inverse result occurs. In a fascinating experiment, when given a reward (playing with a Polaroid camera) before they started, children told less creative stories. However, when they were left to play with the camera without it being contingent on their story-telling performance, their creativity was not affected; in other words, when it was not perceived as *either* a 'please' or 'thank you' reward. This further confirms the need for intrinsic pleasure in the task itself to enhance creativity. The surprise is how finely tuned psychologically creative people are for these innocuous differences to have such a subconscious effect. Equally surprising is the fact that this seemingly subtle tendency, like creativity itself, is found in children.

Information or interference

More recent research has found that in some conditions extrinsic motivators can have a positive influence on creativity. In one experiment, subjects were told how to succeed or 'be creative' on a particular kind of task and were rewarded for carrying out these behaviours. Most of this kind of work utilizes standard creativity tests, and thus incorporates the attributes of original-ity, fluidity, flexibility and elaboration. When subjects were told that originality was measured on how *unusual* responses were – a simple clarification of 'originality' – their originality when rated rose. They had accepted this as useful information, rather than an instruction, or interference. Little of this research has been translated into creativity training methods even in the most progressive companies.

The earlier example in which women students made a collage was more open-ended, and no help as to what was meant by creativity was given. However, when, in that experiment, students were give guidance on how to create a collage that would be rated as creative by judges, it was found that actual creativity increased. Once again, once the 'interference' was construed as helpful learning or information *to be creative* and to be used or not used, it no longer had a detrimental effect on creativity.

In a variation of the Polaroid camera reward experiment, a group of children was shown a video of other children discussing intrinsic motivation and the way they could distance themselves from outside interference to focus on and enjoy the task. In this case the detrimental effects of extrinsic rewards were eliminated and the group shown the video produced higher levels of creativity.

Clearly, the creative person wants to be more competent, and especially more creative. They will gladly accept guidance if it 'comes across' as guidance, rather than a constraint on their freedom to create. They will accept information if it helps to do what they want to do and be what they want to be (creative). In summary, perception of control and loss of independence or choice inhibits creativity.

Workplace motivation

In the workplace, rewards in the form of an environment and facilities more conducive to creativity can have a beneficial effect, just like the helpful guidance given to students making a collage. In this case, the support of the company is seen, not as a reward for creativity, but as assisting that end. We shall see in Chapter 13 that sometimes a creative department is physically separated or treated as a separate organization hierarchically to give this semblance of autonomy. In monetary terms, this may be an expensive 'reward' to achieve creativity and not without other kinds of detrimental spin-offs in the organization. But based on what we have seen from the research it would not be as detrimental to real *creative output* as would, say, prizes or bonuses for the most original product ideas, or a bigger desk. Measured in terms of the crucial need for continual creative outputs, and over the longer term, the more radical structural solution may prove to be the best investment. That is, getting the *conditions* and organizational *culture* right and leaving creativity to the people. Creativity is an individual rather than an organizational phenomenon, and the basic rule seems to be to insulate the individual from the detrimental effects of being part of an endemically 'left-brain' organization.

CQ motivation

We can learn from motivational research to increase our personal creativity. The research findings apply not just with creative people but ordinary people doing creative things. So the phenomena surrounding creative behaviour are common. More than that, we can do something about them so that they have the effect we prefer, rather than do their work unconsciously. Just as *awareness* of an annoying habit may be enough for us to stop it, simple *awareness* of the irrationality of allowing external factors to affect us reduces their otherwise detrimental effect. As you understand the potential positive effects of external motives, they may provide additional motivation over and above intrinsic motivation. Better still, you can draw upon information and guidance to increase your creativity and enjoy the task even more.

Perception

Our perception of external motivators is what matters. Creative performers such as dancers and actors, whilst engrossed in their internal creative performance, learn to appreciate and draw upon positive feedback from the audience. The creative geniuses of history were not all without egos and immune to extrinsic incentives. However, in some cases, 'recognition' was for them the acceptance of a theory or idea by peers and a new or enlarged domain rather then public acclaim or a material reward. Some, however, such as painters, depended on commissions from wealthy people. In such cases, as with facilities provided today by a company to foster creativity among staff, extrinsic motivation directly supported or was complementary to their prime motive of pursuing their chosen work. Such 'rewards', it seems, are acceptable.

Highly creative scientists in particular are known to have a strong desire for recognition that seems to be linked to their intrinsic commitment to their work. The problems they identify, for instance, may be things they are dissatisfied with in the domain, and they need recognition for the legitimacy of undertaking controversial and what may appear to be misguided enquiries. Of course these perceptions are subjective, and different stage performers may have different feelings abut the same audience or may value peer recognition higher than audience applause. Simple neuro-linguistic programming techniques can change these and any subjective perceptions, so extrinsic constraints need be no barrier to personal creativity. With intrapersonal intelligence, or self-awareness, you will be aware of the subjectivity and 'negotiability' of your perceptions and can choose to think and behave differently.

Synergy

But even this differentiation of extrinsic motivators does not tell the full story. Different stages in the creative process respond differently to intrinsic and extrinsic motivators. Where novelty is crucial, only intrinsic motivation will produce the originality needed. This also applies in any open-ended creative activity such as generating the problem ('what is the question?') or suggesting several potential solutions or lines of enquiry. However, *synergistic* extrinsic motivators may help towards the eventual creative product. For example, as part of a task or project preparation, a person may have to absorb a lot of information and learn new skills, both of which demand dogged persistence rather than originality and 'ideational fluidity'. This is subject to ordinary extrinsic motivators. Likewise, once a problem has been cracked by an inspired insight, ordinary rewards may then help to maintain interest in less challenging work as findings are verified and communicated.

Control

From these examples it is clear that we need to differentiate between different kinds of extrinsic motivators. These have been classified, for instance, as having either control or 'information' effects. Where a reward is perceived as control, creativity will be reduced. Where a reward is perceived as information, it will not affect, or may enhance, creativity. Your perception will either help or hinder your CQ aspirations.

Another classification is as between synergistic extrinsic motivators and non-synergistic extrinsic motivators. The former provide information and help the person to complete a task better, and they work in concert with intrinsic motivators in increasing the pleasure gained from the work itself. The latter may lead the person to feel they are controlled, and these work counter to intrinsic motives. Synergistic extrinsic motivators can be particularly effective when intrinsic motivation is already high. Put another way, if you love what you do, other things seem to go right and you are 'on a roll'.

A highly creative person may be no different to anyone else in the way that they respond to carrots and sticks: it is just that their essentially creative traits require intrinsic motives if they are to remain fresh and productive. By purposely building in appropriate rewards for the kinds of work for which we need extrinsic motivation, you can improve your overall creativity production – seeing far more tasks and ideas through to fruition. Likewise, by relaxation techniques and 'anchoring' past creative moments in which you were intrinsically motivated, you can do better in the truly creative aspects of your life.

11

Measuring creativity

We associate measuring psychological traits and processes with pen and paper questionnaires and psychometrics. During the first golden age of creativity – the quarter century or so after Guilford's rallying cry to the American Psychological Association in 1950 – psychometric approaches to the study of creativity dominated the research. However, much of the work was linked to psychometric work on intelligence, and its relationship to creativity, rather than creativity per se. Intelligence quotient (IQ) in particular, with its different scientific camps, dominated psychometrics and creativity psychometrics have flourished in its wake. But for whatever reason, creativity has been an important part of the development of psychometric research, and remains so. For most people, the idea of increasing their thinking ability will be linked to the idea of measurement and questionnaires, and concepts such as IQ and EQ. Even though we can question the extent to which some cognitive abilities are measurable – if at all – it comes down to 'mental measurement', or psychometrics.

Psychometrics

In fact psychometrics dates from well before the 1950 watershed. Francis Galton, for example, called attention to the measurement of creativity in his 1883 *Inquiries into Human Faculty*. Binet and Henri developed divergent thinking tests before 1900, and about the same time Whipple worked on tests of imagination and invention. Further examples appear during the *Human Engineering Laboratories* of the 1930s and 1940s. For a while the dominance of behaviourism kept psychometric research into creativity on the back burner until it was resurrected on a grand scale. Now the tables have turned and the dominance of the psychometric approach has accounted for most research into creativity during the same post-1950 period.

A lot of doubt has been cast on the validity of measures of creativity, a concept, as we have seen, yet to be satisfactorily defined. Nevertheless, psychometric tests are used routinely as the basis for other forms of experimental research into creativity that we have already discussed, such as the effect of the environment (Chapters 8 and 9) or the relationship to intelligence (Chapter 7). For better or worse – and nothing better has come to light – creativity tests generally have greatly influenced our present understanding of creativity. Many people think that creativity is indefinable and not measurable anyway, and the inherent difficulty in measuring it must raise questions as to how far the psychometric approach can be taken.

The recent advances in biometric approaches referred to in Chapter 3 – measuring actual brain activity whilst carrying out creative processes – might prove to be timely. But this and other approaches have their own problems. The question remains as to what exactly is being measured, in particular how synaptic-level changes relate to high-level creative outputs such as ideas – bridging the gulf between the brain and the mind. Or what creative products we should choose as examples of creativity, and take account of the effect of the culture and environment. This brings us back to definition, not just of 'creativity' holistically, but of purportedly measurable characteristics such as originality, fluency and flexibility which individual tests address.

The tests differ a lot, however, in the conditions under which they are taken. Some are in the form of a game rather than a test, so there is less pressure. Some have strict time limits, while others do not impose any limit at all. These factors affect results, of course, and any scientific work based upon them. Some have argued that timed tests do not reflect the real characteristics of insightful thinking as witnessed in the real world. For example, you can't order a 'eureka' to a work problem by five o'clock. The time pressure, or even a 'test' environment, can make an otherwise creative person dry up.

Similarly, different results occur when students are *asked* specifically to 'be creative', or think of novel answers, and given preliminary training, as compared to being given general instructions for completing the questionnaire. None of these factors means necessarily that we cannot measure in some respects, nor that the various tests are not valid in some of the limited things they do. But the cognitive science of psychometrics has not yet arrived at any stable, standardized measure of creativity, or CQ.

Creativity tests

Creativity tests are now becoming as popular as IQ tests. You can test your own creativity on the Internet and in some cases download free tests. There is a specimen test at the end of the chapter. You will notice that the questions simply reflect the basic characteristics of creativity we have covered in the book, so you can check for yourself whether, on average, you fit the factors. You have met a couple of the questions already in the book.

Most of these tests are not validated scientifically and there is no standard measure, or 'CQ'. They are mainly fun exercises and simply apply the characteristics we have discussed throughout the book in question form. You could probably design a more comprehensive test of your own. We have already seen why a reliable creativity quotient in quantitative form is not possible. However, these various tests can help to pinpoint the specific characteristics of creativity that we are not so hot on. Averaged out, and in terms of which quartile you slot into, they may also approximate your rating on the features of creative thinking covered – such as components of divergent thinking. Moreover, practice in the form of test taking is better than none at all, although real life offers hundreds of opportunities every day to exercise your creative mind.

The tests used in psychometric research are more reliable than downloadable ones, including the proprietary ones you pay for. More formal tests themselves must undergo basic tests. The fact that these 'tests of tests' have not been fully met explains why no creativity quotient as universal as IQ (despite its shortcomings) has been developed. These are none the less criteria that need to be applied if the test results are to have scientific credibility. Four main criteria are usually applied.

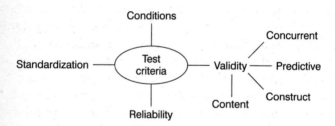

Standardization

Procedures need to be standardized, and this extends not just to the questions, but also to the test-taking conditions and environment. This applies to any sort of test instrument, but creativity involves special conditions that are particularly difficult to maintain. For example, creative insights often occur when a person is alone (or at least anonymous and undisturbed in a crowd) and in a relaxed state of mind, with no distractions. So ordinary distractions that might be acceptable when doing logical IQ-type tests may not be acceptable when the unconscious mind needs to be activated. Insights can also occur at any time (or not at all for a day or a week) and not within standardized time parameters of tests. On the face of it, the special demands of creativity seem to preclude normal experimental conditions, and therefore the validity and standardization of tests.

Test conditions

Test conditions, such as the perceived degree of formality or informality, will affect the outcome of a test, whether implicit or explicit. As we saw in the previous chapter, there is plenty of evidence that the instructions before the test have a major effect on performance. For example, whether the test takers are asked to be creative, told not to be afraid of making mistakes, assured that answers cannot be 'wrong' and so on. Even the implicit tone or ambience of the test environment, the style and personality of the supervisor, the explicit or implicit dress norms, and suchlike will have an effect – probably different from person to person. Little more than room temperature and physical layout can be controlled to scientific method standards (even though they usually are not). All this makes the words on a questionnaire seem relatively simple aspects of standardization by comparison – which is far from the case. These imponderables also help to show why creativity doesn't fit well with psychometric testing and the idea of a precise quotient.

Timing is an important aspect of test conditions. Creativity doesn't respond to a deadline, yet few tests allow unlimited time. Most have a time limit and thus the connotation of real tests and school examinations. These constraints are inconsistent with what we know about the factors that enhance creative thinking. In fact a time limit is one of the best ways to generate the very stress that prevents creative thought. It precludes a spontaneous insight that happens to miss closing time.

Reliability

The reliability criterion means that the same test should get similar results when retaken at a later date, and remain valid with different people in different places and as against other forms of the test. In short, results should be comparable on a like-for-like basis around the world and over time. This is clearly subject to the need for standardization just discussed, whether in timing, environmental conditions, or instructions and guidelines. The reliability of even the most popular creativity tests has been questioned in important research.

Validity

The test should be valid insofar as it measures what it is supposed to measure. It involves the design of the tests, the characteristics or other variables measured, the way the questions are phrased – in short, the 'integrity' of the test instrument. The following criteria are usually applied to validity:

- *Content*. Content validity refers to the questions and type of questions. Do they truly measure the creativity characteristics that the test is designed to identify?
- *Construct*. This involves the design of the test, and whether it does what is intended. It reflects, for example, whether the components, such as originality and flexibility, represent the hypothetical 'creativity' being measured.
- *Predictive*. This relates to whether it will predict what it is intended to – such as future creative 'products' and other evidence of creativity.
- *Concurrent*. Do results correlate with other equivalent tests designed to measure the same thing? This will confirm or otherwise the construct validity.

These test criteria illustrate why we cannot depend on correct psychometric methods. The difficulty lies in the multiple problems of:

- defining creativity;
- agreeing on its component traits;
- measuring external factors such as the culture;

- accounting for personal factors such as motivation;
- controlling subjective behaviour in laboratory conditions;
- capturing the unpredictable, spontaneous creative events such as 'illumination'.

Self-testing

You can apply the information in earlier chapters to measure your own creativity qualitatively over a period. The psychometric test questions used are simply based on the characteristics we have met and you can compose similar questions yourself, such as to measure fluidity. Or you can expand on the type of questions in a downloaded test to obtain a more representative score (but check that the questions reflect the characteristics we have identified based on proper research). Originality is a bit trickier as a DIY task as it involves statistical methods, but even this is measured subjectively by judges in some research.

By monitoring your creativity on a day-to-day basis rather than in artificial test conditions you will get a far better idea of your CQ, or the extent to which you are using your potential creativity. Most importantly, you can record spontaneous creative events that can only be captured on a 24-hour basis. This is a good reason for keeping a creativity journal. Often people find that they start to experience far more creative events, and that their quality, or the significance in terms of their personal goals, increases. Similarly, what may have been rare period of flow, as we discussed in Chapter 5, may become a regular part of your life. Each aspect of creativity that we have covered – the processes, the personal traits and characteristics, the wider systems that play a part – will help to raise your creative thinking profile. Specific relaxation and 'downtime' practice (Chapter 5) will especially add to your creative thinking skills. If appropriate, belief change exercises using neurolinguistic programming will pave the way for faster progress if you have up to now not seen yourself as a creative person.

Informal creativity questionnaires and online tests are for fun only, or practice. Formal tests such as Torrance's, although used widely in education and research, are not standardized and their validity continues to be questioned. You can appreciate this as you compare the wider criteria we have covered in the book and the criteria for validity earlier in this chapter. They measure divergent thinking only and do not reflect important characteristics such as motivation – as we have seen, a crucial factor in much of the research. Self-monitoring, over a period, based on all the traits and processes you have learnt will help you to understand both the nature of creativity and your own in particular. You will find that your creativity increases in quantity and quality (CQ) and you should be able to identify creative products. Specific conditioning exercises such as relaxation and alpha state generation will also help, as will a whole variety of techniques once you establish your self-belief as a creative person and realize your potential.

What the tests measure

Creativity tests, by and large, measure the various characteristics that have been associated with creative people, processes and products. As we have seen, these are numerous. They comprise 'personality' traits, such as risk taking or independence, as well as more specific cognitive characteristics such as divergent thinking. The psychometric challenge therefore has been:

■ to select a manageable short list of characteristics that, together, if exhibited by an individual, would constitute creativity;

■ to design questions to establish that these characteristics exist and quantify them;

■ to standardize the tests and make them valid and reliable, per the 'tests of tests' above.

The scale of such a task can first be appreciated in the volume and variety of creativity characteristics, and in their difficulty to define to a level that allows measurement. The following list, although not exhaustive, will underline the subjective nature of these characteristics and the difficulty of precise, quantitative (as a CQ) measurement:

- Sensitivity to problems.
- Word fluency. Can state words containing a given letter or number of letters.
- Associational fluency. Can easily state synonyms for a given word.
- Expressional fluency. Can easily write well-formed sentences with a specified content.
- Ideational fluency. Can easily think of ideas to meet certain requirements, such as to name things with given properties such as hard, soft, edible, or decide on a suitable title for a given story.
- Spontaneous flexibility. Can produce a large variety of ideas, such as uses for a brick or paper clip.
- Originality, shown as producing ideas statistically unlikely.
- Making remote associations – that is, between things remote in time or space or logically.
- Giving responses that are judged to be 'clever', as well as original.
- Redefinition. That is, the ability to abandon old associations of familiar objects and use them in new ways. For example, which of the following objects could best be used to make a needle: pencil, radish, shoe, fish, carnation? (fish – use bone).
- Elaboration. That is, the ability to fill in details given a general scheme. For example, given two lines or a simple geometric shape, create a more complicated object.
- Tolerance of ambiguity. This means willingness to accept uncertain information or conclusions, not being confined to rigid categories.

- ■ Interest in convergent thinking – towards one correct answer. We saw that the total creative process includes critical appraisal of ideas to meet certain constraints.
- ■ Interest in divergent thinking. Open-minded thinking, where there is no single correct answer. The ability to envisage multiple solutions to a problem.

Divergent thinking

The main feature in creativity psychometrics is divergent thinking and the best-known tests are Guilford's *Structure of the Intellect* (SOI) divergent production tests, Torrance's *Test of Creative Thinking* (TTCT) and those of Wallach and Kogan, and Getzels and Jackson, respectively. These are all in wide use, both in creativity research and education. The TTCT, based on many features of the SOI, is the most commonly used divergent thinking test and is used internationally.

There are several dozen such tests comprising the various divergent thinking components of Guilford's SOI model. The battery of tests covers:

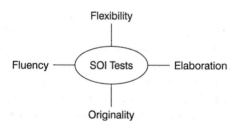

These are the main components of divergent thinking we met earlier:

- ■ fluency – number of ideas;
- ■ flexibility – variety of perspectives;
- ■ originality – or statistical infrequency;
- ■ elaboration of ideas – beyond that required by the prompt.

An adaptation of the SOI battery of tests, the *Structure of the Intellect Learning Abilities Test* (SOI-LA), diagnoses weaknesses in divergent thinking, which are then addressed by remedial training.

Both Getzels and Jackson and Wallach and Kogan developed similar tests. The *Instances Test*, for example, asks students to list as many things that move on wheels, that make a noise, etc as possible. You can create this popular sort of creativity exercise yourself and practise it to your heart's content. You can even monitor your improvement over a period. Not only does this foster creativity, but you actually create the *habit* of thinking that way, which is the crucial requirement for *being* creative as compared with *acting creatively* (which you need to do anyway).

Creating mental habits in this way is not mind over matter. As we saw in the chapter on the brain, your brain literally forms new neural pathways and synaptic connections. It then reconfigures itself as a whole to continuously re-create the new 'you'. From that moment your brain has more to draw upon when it produces those amazing associations, brainwaves, ready-made solutions and leaps of logic. Mental habits are the *processes* you use, or the *patterns* of thought involved in an attitude or personality trait.

There is no limit to the extent to which you can demonstrate fluidity and originality, and it is this potential that provides the challenge in divergent thinking. When you match the increasingly challenging task with your increasing ability, the process – at any level – soon becomes easy and habitual. It is a different way to look at the world and to approach work. Top sports people make what they do so easy, and economy of effort is a sign of true expertise. In some cases it seems they cannot reach the highest levels of skill without controlling their mental state and stimulating flow experiences.

Evaluating creativity

Creativity-testing instruments for the most part amount to divergent thinking tests, and so cover just that aspect of creativity. For example, there is less emphasis on measuring the preparation and evaluation stages in the creative process, or what we described earlier as the more left-brain elements. Divergent thinking instruments tend to capture fluidity and flexibility. However, it is hard to imagine how standard psychometric tests could capture the spontaneous insights that characterize creativity, the basic mental incubation process, or just sitting gazing at nothing, yet producing worthwhile ideas and occasionally a ground-breaking insight. People are unpredictable enough as scientific subjects, but here we have one of the most unpredictable and incomprehensible aspects of human behaviour.

Final creative products are usually the result of a choice based on some sort of evaluation. Expert judges are commonly used. It has been argued therefore that research on fluidity of ideas (ideational fluidity) has been at the expense of research on the appropriateness or utility of those ideas, and the extent to which they will result in 'culturally valued products'. Insight is likewise given less attention than fluidity. Although the illumination or inspiration stage appears in most models of the creative process, it has not been captured in tests.

Insight

The absence or uneven weighting of different creativity traits in psychometric instruments partly reflects the experimental difficulties involved. As we have seen, it also reflects the thorny problem of definition. Insight questions are thus lacking and are more likely to be used as parlour games or on creativity seminars where they help to create interest. The problem with insight questions is that they have to be designed to be answered within a reasonable time and within the constraints of test conditions. Usually we experience an insight in the shower, when driving, out walking or when doing something quite different to the subject of the illuminated problem in mind. Insights, because they have an interesting, surprising, non-logical twist (or they would not be termed 'insight'), tend to be both surprising and, depending on the quality and circumstances, memorable. Some stereotypical examples, like the nine-point square, crop up in dozens of creativity textbooks, so they are of little use in tests as some of the test-takers are sure to have met them before. Others, like the Necker cube, as well as illustrating the mental processes, can provide practice in switching rapidly between different ways of seeing something – in effect from one neural pattern to another in the brain. There are four views; two with the spot at the front face, nearest you at top right and bottom left, and two with the spot on the back face of the cube in the same positions. The views are from a little above to the right, and a little below to the left. Try to switch views in split seconds. Then see it as a two-dimensional hexagonal pattern with the dot in the centre.

Once students are familiar with the fairly limited examples of what may seem like trick questions, they will no longer require insight to answer them. So it is questionable whether they measure true insight, test familiarity, good preparation and the common sense to make such preparation, or a good memory. Thus, on the occasions that insight questions are included in a psychometric test they do little for its validity, which may be shaky to start with. You can prepare for the fairly limited range of insight-type test questions just as you can rehearse for an IQ test (if you are into boosting your IQ my book *Boost your Intelligence* covers that specifically). But test familiarity does not reveal true creativity, although it may be a measure of a person's judgement and common sense – part of the truer definition of intelligence.

Personality traits

Psychometric questionnaires also cover personality characteristics, focusing more on the person rather than the process. The *Inventory for Finding Talent*, *Group Inventory for Finding Interests*, 'What Kind of Person are You', *Adjective Check List* (in part), and the *16 Personality Factor Questionnaire* are examples. These typically have a creativity *component*, although expressed in different terms such as 'explorer'.

Personality traits are perhaps more significant in creativity research when they relate to people known to be highly creatively productive – as when measuring the effect of personality type on creative products. In this way it has been confirmed that the personality characteristics of creative people include:

- originality;
- independence;
- risk taking;
- curiosity;
- energy;
- attraction to complexity and novelty;
- artistic sense;
- open-mindedness;
- need for privacy.

Another interesting trait in highly creative people – perhaps at the level of identity or self-image – is the awareness of their own creativity. These are some of the long-term traits we can emulate or 'model'. In some cases you may find that you exercise a certain trait in another part of your life, even in a narrow interest or hobby. In that case you can use vividly recalled memories of the state as a resource to apply to parts of your life that could benefit from such states, and the confidence that goes with them. You can 'anchor' these (see Chapter 14) so that they will trigger at the time and in the circumstances you need them, to be more creative. Or you can imagine someone you know who has the trait you desire and imagine what they would think and do in the same circumstance. This is an innate skill we all had as children and you can easily refresh it if you want to rekindle your creativity.

The advantage of using personality tests such as the 16 PF is that they have proven validity at the level of personality – they measure what is intended. The disadvantage is that the creativity elements, if present (as some omit recognizable creative characteristics), differ from test to test and suffer from the same weaknesses as divergent thinking tests.

Popular psychometric creativity tests

A few psychometric creativity instruments have been widely adopted and are in turn the basis for other aspects of creativity research. A lot therefore hinges on their validity, and this accounts for doubts among scientists as to whether psychometrics and experimental creativity work can be called 'science'. There is far less doubt, however, about the various factors that go to make up tests. These are more important to the person who personally wants to improve their creativity. Moreover, the area in which the tests have at least internal validity – they do what they are designed to do even though they are not generalizable to the outside world – is divergent thinking, which is without doubt an important part of the creativity package. Familiarity with the test questions is useful for the person who needs to build up their confidence in their innate creativity before embarking on projects that the world (their 'system') will evaluate. Using the tests in a training context will provide a hands-on introduction to different features of creative thinking.

Structure of Intellect (SOI)

Guilford's SOI divergent production test is one of the earliest of the divergent thinking batteries. It sets out to measure divergent thinking in various areas:

- ■ *semantic units* (eg consequences of not needing to eat);
- ■ *figural classes* (eg finding as many classifications of sets of figures as possible);
- ■ *figural units* (elaborating on simple figures such as a circle or square to make meaningful pictures).

There are dozens of tests derived from the SOI model, and others have produced their version of it, such as the *Structure of Intellect-Learning Abilities Test* (SOI-LA).

Torrance Test of Creative Thinking (TTCT)

This is probably the most popular series and is in wide use in research and education. It is based on many of the SOI battery of tests. Students provide multiple responses to word and picture prompts and these are measured for fluidity, flexibility, originality and elaboration – features we have already met. The administration and scoring of these tests have been improved over the years, partially in an ongoing attempt to counter criticisms of validity as new research is undertaken. Like IQ tests, if it is judged for what it measures rather than what it doesn't measure, it is a useful tool – and about the best around anyway.

Instances Test

This test is similar to the SOI and asks students to list as many things as possible that float, make a noise, etc. The *Uses Test* variation asks them to identify all the different ways you could use an object (eg chair, paper clip, brick, potato).

Other tests

Various other tests of creativity that appear widely are:

- ■ providing the ending to a story;
- ■ identifying embedded figures;
- ■ interpreting similar patterns.

Biometric testing

Psychometrics is not the only form of cognitive measurement. Biometric, or 'neurometric' creativity testing involves actual electro-chemical brain measurements and is a latecomer in the research. Until recently, it got little attention in the widespread psychometric encampments. As is often the case, technology has helped to advance this approach. Techniques include the monitoring by computerized scanning of a subject's glucose metabolism in the brain while they carry out different creative activities. Glucose level indicates brain activity so tests can show which parts of the brain are activated.

We need not concern ourselves with the technology of converting brain activity into pictures or lines on a graph, but rather with what this reveals about the processes and the credibility it gives to what previously had not been subject to such direct measurement. By varying tasks and conditions, experiments can show what sort of activities and environments produce or hinder such brain patterns. The scanning evidence particularly shows the different processes happening in parallel that reflect the well-known holistic and detailed perspectives on any mental operation.

The biometric approach suffers from the same difficulties of deciding what is a creative task, as well as imprecise measurement. As scanning technology improves there will be increasing scope for these methods. They may provide a much-needed reconciliation stage between the Cartesian mind-level studies and the neurophysiological research at the micro neuronal level. An important aim will be to capture the random 'eureka' and 'flow' experiences that are characteristic of creativity. Another aim will be to create specific states by biofeedback methods, as has been successfully done with inducing the alpha brain state.

Biometric tests are used in empirical research rather than as an IQ-type individual scoring mechanism, not least because of the great cost involved in PET and MRI scanning processes. Pen and paper tests, with their equivalent online version, remain the main form of psychometric testing.

Tests on tests

We listed above some of the criteria for test validity and these are by no means consistently met, or even incorporated into research design. The plethora and popularity of creativity tests can easily hide their many weaknesses. To attain any level of credibility, predictability would have to be shown. For example, a child's test rating might predict future creative products such as skill in playing a musical instrument or in visual art. This is not unreasonable – even IQ tests can predict academic performance and other indices of success (even if not reflecting 'intelligence'). However, psychometric research is not the easiest kind of scientific project. We need to measure creativity over long periods (in longitudinal studies) and there are plenty of cases where a person's creativity is not recognized until long after they are dead. It is also common for people to take up creative hobbies in retirement that they did not find the time for when younger.

Experimental research hurdles

The following is a brief summary of the main hurdles we face in experimental research into creativity and met earlier in the context of psychometric studies.

Prediction

The timescale problem still begs the question of what precisely is being predicted. Hence the key question, what are the criteria which we need to test, and which will predict the creative productivity of a person at some time in the future? We have seen that a whole range of criteria play some part in what makes a person creative, rather than the short list usually selected for a test questionnaire. Ideally we need to test for them all, as any one, such as motivation or early childhood encouragement, could be significant. But at the same time we would need to know which – if any – accounted for different kinds of creative production in the future. In that way we could intervene and train in the crucial characteristics. Or we could direct training to particular creative products such as musical skill, business enterprise or a sport.

Personality

As we have seen, typically, a short list of criteria are used in the psychometric instruments, such as fluidity, flexibility, originality and elaboration. But this excludes the personality, or long-term personal traits also traditionally associated with creative people. We have referred in the book to risk taking, independence and suchlike. Like motivation and family influences, one or two of these traits might tip the balance in bringing about creative products later in a person's lifetime. However, they need to be isolated to show that they are independent of the other characteristics such as fluidity and originality.

Product

We then need to define a creative product, or the criteria that will be evidence of creativity. Many popular measures, such as registered patents, may call upon administrative and interpersonal skills as much as true creativity. This is especially so if we have no adequate method for rating patents for their creative content – that is, for quality rather than (as is the measure usually adopted) quantity. The same problem applies to published scientific papers, new products introduced, musical compositions or works of art.

Motivation

An even bigger weakness is that motivation is not controlled. We have seen that this is usually a major factor in a person's creative output over the years, as well as in experimental tasks in a research study. Even rewards do not produce the *intrinsic* motivation essential for creative thinking. Moreover, the source of motivation will differ widely and may be lost in the mists of childhood.

Control vs. spontaneity

Chapter 12 on experimental research underlines the almost insurmountable problem of deciding on and controlling all the variables. In particular, the need for human subjects means that standardization, consistency and even reasonable predictability of behaviour in response to a given stimulus are probably unattainable. People, and especially creative people, are just like that. But in the field of creativity even that is not the core problem. The nature of creativity is about spontaneity, unpredictability and uniqueness – surprises. So even in controlled conditions replicability would seem to be inconsistent with originality and spontaneity. Unlike samples of chemicals, it is hard to get like samples of human beings. Unless on a massive scale, random choice of subjects is unlikely to take account of their variable personality characteristics, native culture, childhood background and intrinsic motivation. Motivation may be the single most uncontrollable of all the common criteria applied to creativity, but any missing variable would skew the findings.

Psychometric measurement difficulties need not be a problem, however, if you want to boost your CQ. It does, though, show the value and significance of findings that are eventually made, the caveats to apply, and the need for more knowledge. Motivation, for example, is just a mental pattern or strategy that can be modelled, either on another part your life (in which you have more confidence and creative expression) or on another person, and 'installed' as a habit. Most people know the interests that motivate them, so can develop greater creativity in these areas before installing motives that do not exist. Taking up a wider range of interests and behaviour will, in any case, throw up exciting challenges from time to time that are ripe for creative thinking. You can make these sorts of life changes easily, one by one. If negative beliefs are deep seated you can use the belief change processes covered in my book *The Ultimate How To Book* (Gower). Otherwise, simply by *acting out* the creativity processes and traits we have covered you will find that your self-belief as a 'creative person' grows, especially as you produce evidence in the form of creative products.

Moving target

From the increase in quasi-scientific studies it may appear that capital C Creativity is waiting to be defined and finally measured, and applied for the advancement of civilization. However, a static concept of creativity may be quite wrong. We have seen that it is as much a social as a psychological or biological construct, dependent on the recognition of peers in a domain of expertise, and the wider culture. We saw also that even the culture – let alone the changing fashions of a narrow domain – is a changing entity and a moving target. Historiometrics, whilst seemingly even further from a modern scientific approach than quasi-scientific psychometric studies, makes a strong case for the cultural influence on, if not nature of, creativity. Unless we see creativity as a moving target with contemporary, cultural overtones, we might suss out Einstein's creativity but be left guessing when it comes to computer-literate 10-year-olds in our own generation.

Without objective measures of creative outputs perhaps the control of input criteria is of academic interest anyway. What each approach shows us, however, is a list of human characteristics that together spell creativity. This applies whether we look at personality traits in the *person* or the characteristics reflected in a *process*. Pragmatically, this is the list you need to get to grips with if you want to be more creative in your life. Ask yourself, for example:

■ How can I think outside the box?
■ How can I see things from other points of view?
■ How can I be less concerned about authority?
■ How can I maintain focus on the job in hand?
■ How can I find pleasure and fulfilment in anything I do?

You will no doubt have your own questions. We have evidence that some of these criteria are amenable to DIY influences, stimuli and straightforward practice and conditioning. For example, alpha feedback training is known to enhance some aspects of creativity and even the most difficult subjects can benefit to some degree. Relaxation generally has also been linked to some of the creativity criteria short list and this also is readily learnable. A range of 'provocation' techniques can boost creativity in the case of actual problems. Better still, if you use these regularly they will be come habits.

However, for some important aspects of creativity, training in the conventional sense does not seem to apply. For example, the inspiration and 'breakthrough' parts of a wider process that catches the popular imagination seems to be outside our control altogether, let alone teachable. Put another way, a repeatable, systematized, formula-type or 'three-point' approach, by definition, does not fit the somewhat anarchic ways of true creativity. The Muse might not speak until long after the 5 pm seminar finishing time. More general mental conditioning, however, can be likened to general fitness training for an athlete as a foundation for more technical training.

Such creativity enhancement is quite feasible. For example, you can change your self-belief as a creative person, attitude, and mental state to facilitate the spontaneity and originality you aim for. Given awareness, understanding and an appropriate attitude to training, the many techniques available will find a more fertile brain in which to work. The difficulties of researching and measuring creativity need not bother us as individuals. At the same time we benefit from what we can learn about characteristics and processes. The questions that have been developed in the best instruments, such as Torrance's, will help to pinpoint the specific characteristics you should aim for, among others we have covered in the book. The factors that the tests cannot cope with you can monitor and stimulate yourself, making use of a journal and what you have learnt in the book. There is much still to learn about being creative, but there need be no mystery about the practical benefits. By applying what you know now you can increase your CQ and be more productive in the direction of life you choose.

Creativity self-assessment

A. Self-assessment

1. Do you consider yourself creative?
   - a. Very
   - b. Moderately
   - c. Not at all
2. What creative accomplishments have you achieved in the past?
   - a. Many
   - b. Some
   - c. None
3. Do you want to be more creative?
   - a. Yes
   - b. No
4. Do you think it's your destiny to develop something creatively?
   - a. Yes
   - b. No
5. When you were growing up, did the following apply?
   - a. Moved frequently
   - b. Given freedom and independence to think for yourself
   - c. Given clear standards of right and wrong
   - d. Parents were independent and effective in their work
   - e. Parents respected you and your abilities
   - f. Intense closeness was avoided
   - g. Consistent and effective discipline
   - h. Many positive models to identify with
   - i. Lack of pressure to find professional identity
   - j. Parents had more artistic, cultural, and intellectual interests than neighbours
6. Do you
   - a. allow free time during the day to do nothing?
   - b. feel guilty when not working?
   - c. alternate between work and play?

7. Do you love the work that you want to be creative?
   - a. Yes
   - b. No
8. Do you ask questions that might seem stupid to others?
   - a. Yes
   - b. No
9. Do you
   - a. 'Strike while the iron is hot?'
   - b. 'Make the iron hot by striking?'
   - c. 'Strike out?'
10. Do you believe?
    - a. 'If it ain't broke, don't fix it'
    - b. 'It's always broke'
11. Do you
    - a. need a logical explanation for everything?
    - b. delight in uncertainty and mystery?
12. Do you
    - a. prefer to work alone?
    - b. prefer to work in groups?
13. Do you
    - a. need to put everything in its proper place?
    - b. tolerate ambiguous situations well?
14. In problem solving do you
    - a. need to have a clear plan before moving ahead?
    - b. try anything to find a direction to move?
15. When someone suggests a new idea, do you
    - a. immediately evaluate it, looking for weaknesses?
    - b. defend it, trying to find its strengths?
    - c. play with the possibilities suggested by the idea?
16. In solving problems do you
    - a. logically figure the situation out?
    - b. look for as many possibilities as you can think of?
    - c. rely on hunches that you check out later?
17. Do you believe that intuition is
    - a. a reality worth relying on?
    - b. the inability to be logical?

18. Do you
    - a. like excitement and change?
    - b. prefer peace and a reliable routine?
19. How willing are you to take a chance?
    - a. Comfortable with risking
    - b. Depends upon the situation
20. If you were given a new toy or game to play, would you
    - a. always go by the instructions?
    - b. play around, improvising with the materials?
    - c. devise variations after learning the correct way?
21. Do you agree (A) or disagree (D) with the following?
    - a. What others think about you is important.
    - b. Rules are made to be broken.
    - c. Dreams are useless.
    - d. It's bad to change your mind frequently.
    - e. Wishing makes it happen.
    - f. Curiosity killed the cat.
22. Do you mostly go by
    - a. a situation's potential?
    - b. the practical consequences?
    - c. how others might react?
    - d. the beauty of the solution?

B. Your understanding of creativity

23. Which of the following are characteristics of creativity?
    - a. Spontaneity
    - b. Deliberateness
    - c. Newness
    - d. Value
    - e. Skills
    - f. Play
    - g. Work
    - h. Convergence
    - i. Divergence

24. Does an idea have to be carried out to be considered 'creative'?
    - a. Yes
    - b. No
25. Do you believe creative production
    - a. is best rewarded?
    - b. is hindered by rewards?
26. Do you believe creative behaviour
    - a. is a sign of compensation for unmet emotional needs?
    - b. is an expression of the healthy personality?
27. Creativity
    - a. is an all or none phenomenon – you're creative or you're not?
    - b. exists on a continuum?
28. Which is more important to originality?
    - a. Asking the right question
    - b. Finding the right answer

C. Some challenges

29. Count the squares:

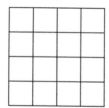

30. Connect the dots with four straight lines:

31. What different uses can you find for a plastic milk bottle?
32. Take a word beginning with 'C'. Then consider the problem of war. Force fit as many metaphoric solutions using your 'C' word. For example, how is war 'cow-like'? 'car-like'? 'candle-like'? What new perspectives can you come up with for solving the problem of war?

Compiled by John G Young MD
djgyoung@uswest.net
http://volusia.com/creative/mag5.htm
Used with permission

12

The quasi-science of creativity

Scientific research doesn't get much more complex than human creativity. The human brain is the most complex organ we have found to date, and creativity – even compared with intelligence – is one of its most awesome and enigmatic characteristics. This reflects itself in the fact that experimental research on creativity is sometimes termed quasi-scientific, especially when compared with the hard sciences. The widespread use of psychometric instruments does not help – they have their own validity problems. Nevertheless, when compared with other forms of research such as historiometrics, relying on archival records of people long since dead, experimental work can appear very scientific in comparison.

Experimental research has played a relatively small part in creativity studies, but the few conclusions are that much more significant for anyone seriously interested in the subject. Even the fact that some aspects of creativity seem outside the scope of scientific method tells us something about the unique nature of human creativity. A deeper interest in this aspect of the subject, rather than the common practice of resorting to techniques, may increase your personal motivation to explore and develop your creative abilities.

The human mind is not the best laboratory to start with, but creativity has its own particular experimental problems. On the positive side, these highlight some of the special characteristics of creative thinking:

- We often associate creativity with unpredictability, yet the whole idea of scientific research is to understand nature by learning its predictable laws and causes and effects.

- Creativity often appears in different domains, such as science, sport or a branch of art, and manifests itself differently. Thus whatever we conclude by experiment may not be generalizable, whether across domains or in the outside world generally.

- If we look on creativity as happening in all our lives although in non-spectacular ways, it becomes impossible to take account of all of the variables that affect our creativity.

- We cannot generalize laboratory discoveries over the physical, cultural, religious etc environments in which creativity takes place.

- Observation is difficult enough but even when we manage it, it brings its own problems. Just being watched may change a subject's responses, for example, and this is especially the case with so-called creative people carrying out creative tasks.

- The specific traits observed may not be the most relevant components of creativity but reflect those that can be more readily subjected to controlled experimentation, tested and validated. These may have far less significance in the total creativity 'package' than less measurable traits such as insight.

- Experiments usually measure creativity by 'proximate' controls, or immediate changes in the variables. Thus the effects of long-term or 'remote' traits in the subjects (such as amenability to risks or dislike of control) are excluded.

Control and complexity

The prime requirement for experimental study of creativity is to be able to control and manipulate the experimental conditions and variables. In the case of the psychometric approach, we focus on the differences that exist between people and the way they do 'creative' tasks. In experimental research, we seek to *induce* changes in individual performance using different interventions – for example, the instructions given about carrying out a particular task. To maintain control, and isolate causes and effects, we need to investigate variables one at a time, starting with the most controllable. In short, we reduce the complexity. However, the more we do this, the more removed is the research from real-life creativity, complex as it may be.

The problem of applying rigorous control over experiments with people, in all their uniqueness and unpredictability, is not just a feature of creativity research, but extends through the 'soft' sciences. As it happens, even laboratory controls such as noise, light, temperature, setting and other unintended distractions are usually lacking, so on the face of it there is plenty of room for more robust study of this subject, however complex.

Spontaneity versus control

Control, however, may be counterproductive, in designing out the very spontaneity that is the essence of creativity. Similarly, creativity usually requires plenty of time, and will certainly not adhere to deadlines, and this runs counter to conventional experimentation. Just how long should an experimenter wait until his or her subject has received that elusive flash of inspiration? How much 'incubation' time needs to be scheduled into the sessions? How do you rate something 'on the tip of your tongue'? Ten per cent or 90 per cent of the solution? You *know* the answer exists, but you also know you cannot force it.

Spontaneity, although a key aspect of creativity, lies well down the list of the traits studied experimentally, and may never be satisfactorily studied at all. In one sense this is inevitable, as spontaneity and control – by their nature – hardly mix. Likewise, we associate creativity with unpredictability, yet we demand of experimental methodology generalizability, predictability and replication. Thus even studies that are internally valid (and duly published in respectable journals) may not be externally valid as they do not properly represent creativity with its myriad of environmental and cultural influences.

People's expressions of creativity are as different as their personalities, experience and cultural background. Thus, in considering the role of experimental research, as against, say, the psychometric or historiometric approaches, we need to consider its contribution overall, with these inbuilt limitations, rather than from individual studies.

Poor relation status

Experimental work on creativity is the poor relation compared with psychometric studies and, in their different heydays, biographical and historiometric approaches. Unfortunately, this may be for the wrong, although obvious, reasons: first, the great difficulty of designing experiments in cognitive areas with behavioural and social dimensions; second, the difficulty of experimentation in particular aspects of creativity, such as spontaneity and unpredictability, that seem incompatible with scientific method. Because these omissions concern key questions, the research we are left with loses credibility in the overall scheme of creativity. Having done that, the top few findings will have particular significance in our understanding and application of creativity

Poor relation status also reflects the definition problem of what exactly is being measured. Just as important, experimental creativity research relies often on standard creativity tests which, as we saw in the previous chapter, themselves are not universally accepted as valid. Experimental work includes measuring the effect of variables or 'interventions' on creative and non-creative subjects based on their test results. This means that we should take experimental findings with a pinch of salt (as most do psychometric findings anyway) but also that experimental findings have greater value because of the stricter methodological controls that have been applied in the research. On top of this, the relatively few firm conclusions probably add scarcity value to laboratory-based studies. The rapid progress in scanning technology also augurs well for experimental as compared with questionnaire-based psychometrics.

The relatively low attention to experimental research may have a more pragmatic reason. Psychometric research into creativity has followed on the coat-tails of intelligence, itself also heavily weighted to psychometrics, and including the popular IQ. So the historical organization of university departments has not found a place for creativity as a stand-alone discipline – it went where intelligence went – and less so for experimental work.

Creativity folklore

Although creativity has received a lot of attention in corporate circles, and increasingly so, this tends to be at the popular, or folklore level, and rarely breaks new ground scientifically. Consequently, hardly any of the popular training programmes adopted by companies and training suppliers have been shown scientifically to give the results they aim for or promise. They are largely harmless, of course, although not necessarily effective, let alone cost-effective. In particular, the emphasis on group and corporate creativity rather than at the individual level misses a lot of what we have found scientifically about creativity.

Lack of academic focus on creativity overall has led to the fragmentation of ideas, definitions and measurement instruments. Paradoxically, creativity, along with genetics, is now widely seen as one of the most important areas of discovery in the coming years. Its secrets will not only help those with hitherto untreatable illnesses, but will allow every one of us to operate at a higher, more fulfilling level of achievement.

Experimental research in creativity is not nearly as extensive as psychometric and historiometric work. This reflects the history of creativity as a 'soft' subject not amenable to scientific methods in the fashion of harder sciences. In fact, it has largely figured in research within the bigger domains of (equally 'soft') 'intelligence' or mystical Cartesian 'mind'.

Experimental manipulation

Simple manipulation of information has been found to affect divergent thinking, creative problem-solving, insight and intuition. Experiments include open-ended, 'real' problems rather than pen and paper or computer-based multiple answers. An open-ended problem used in the research might be how to paint a mile of iron fencing most economically. In some studies, instruction as to 'critical' and 'constructive' evaluation of a task (for a period of time) got different results respectively in the creativity shown. In one case, as well as generating their own ideas, the subjects were informed of common and uncommon examples of solutions. The group that applied constructive criticism to their work (focusing on strengths) produced the most effective solutions. The group that were more critical (focusing on weaknesses) produced more *original* solutions. It was also found that the subjects' attitude changed (as between constructive or critical experimental conditions), and continued through further open-ended (divergent) tests.

Such work is useful in showing the generalizability of the results, and the degree to which creativity may be task-specific, as different kinds of problems were used. It also showed that attitude was not only an important variable in performance, but that it could be manipulated by simple instructions. Perhaps more importantly, it empirically supported the notion that creativity (or in this case originality) can be learnt and stimulated.

'Real' tasks

Different results have been obtained depending on the nature of the tasks. In particular, where tasks are perceived as realistic and useful, greater creativity is displayed than when they are thought to be theoretical or game-like. A real problem, say at work or in personal life, will therefore be a far better basis for measuring creativity than a hypothetical one, but this would remove even the possibility of adequate controls. However, this is important for creativity training, which can utilize live problems without setting out to follow scientific method.

Ownership

'Ownership' of a problem is also important for creative outcomes. One that is owned by the subject or trainee will elicit more attention and motivation than one that is handed down, however challenging the problem may be in its own right. Hence your own personal or work problems are the best basis for CQ training.

Group ownership may apply when a group is acting within the same company towards common objectives. This rarely happens. Individual differences, in commitment to the group or corporate objective and interest in the specific content of the task, are bound to have an effect also. In this light the experimental conclusions above throw doubts upon psychometric tests which deal in 'pretend' problems and tasks. They also underscore the importance of motivation as a key dimension in creativity.

Task information

As we saw in the case of psychometric tests, the instructions given on experimental tasks can affect divergent thinking results in different ways. For instance, flexibility scores have been increased without affecting originality. This suggests that each is a distinct creative characteristic, and that they do not always correlate in an individual's performance. It also shows that flexibility can be manipulated – produced at will through instructions and conditions – although it does not necessarily mean that original ideas will be produced in consequence. Originality needs its own kind of manipulation (or intervention), such as when subjects are told what criteria will apply when results are judged for originality (unusualness or statistical improbability).

The usefulness of instructions varies depending on the human subjects. Non-gifted children benefited more than gifted children, for example. It may be that the gifted children in the studies were already using the strategies that the information supplied. In other cases the information directed subjects to key information that might help results, and again non-gifted children benefited most from the guidance. It seems in this case that the gifted children carried out their own selection process as to what information was relevant or irrelevant in tackling the problem.

Experimental research involving children suggests that too much information might limit creativity. In one case different media were used to give incomplete story information to which the children had to add a story ending. It was found that video (simulating television) produced the lowest creativity, compared with the other media, audio and text. It appears that television and video are too explicit, and contain too much sensory detail, whereas creativity involves filling in information gaps. In the real world we are not presented with a few minutes of canned information, but are surrounded by multi-sensory stimuli too voluminous to be fully assimilated. The unique human skill is to sample this information and make meaning out of it in conjunction with our existing database of experience. It is within this three-dimensional, multi-sensory world that natural creativity happens, and this may explain the tendency in the experiments for subjects to be more creative with sparser information.

Studies involving military personnel showed that instructions as to the best cognitive style to use in problem solving similarly affected results. One study was based on subjects' individual scores under the WAIS questionnaire on the assimilator–explorer axis scale. It was hypothesized that 'assimilators' would extend the problem-solving approach as far as possible, while 'explorers' would vary their problem-solving strategies even when the task did not require such. Besides the instructions as to style increasing the scores, it was found that assimilators benefited from instructions to explore and visualize, and explorers benefited from instructions to analyse.

The conclusion seems to be that, like attitudes discussed earlier, cognitive styles are amenable to change by simple intervention. In short, personal creativity (and indeed analytical skills) can be learnt and improved. Moreover, you do not need a teacher or research scientist to give you instructions, you can use the information from this book. Similarly, you do not need to exhibit your creativity in a controlled environment or through questionnaires, but you can put it to work immediately in every aspect of your life. Depending on what creative 'products' you aspire to, you can measure your own success.

Problem finding

The complex process of sampling the sensory world happens amazingly quickly. Speed of response experiments have been carried on for many years, as speed was for a period considered to be crucial to intelligence and creativity. Speed of processing is particularly associated with creativity. We take in a whole scenario, recalling similar memories and feelings, instantly, such that the process cannot be captured by controlled experiments. This often happens after a period of incubation, so the speed, or flash of inspiration, is what we perceive consciously. The same phenomenon occurs when creative insight seems to jump to a final solution without us knowing – except upon later reflection – the intermediate logical steps to the solution. One instance is in 'problem finding', or problem definition, which has figured in creativity studies. Creative people seem to *redefine the problem* rather than think in terms of a 'solution'. Having done this, the solution seems easy and obvious – especially to others.

In these cases the essential intelligence, or creativity, is in asking the right question, or defining the problem in a way amenable to a better solution. Perhaps this is not so much a matter of speed, but of thinking 'outside the box' – ie creatively. It is simply a more effective way for the brain to handle the problem in question so it seems quick. Children at school are usually *given* problems, rather than being educated to find or create them, and this is no doubt one of the contributors to their gradual loss of creativity throughout school years. The educational system may be economical in staffing and administration, but it must do damage to thinking skills that in many cases is never corrected.

When sticking to conventional problem-solving methods we can easily become fixed in our thinking, and stuck for a solution. The well-used nine-dot square in Chapter 5 is an example of an insight type of problem that illustrates the difference between conventional processing and a creative approach.

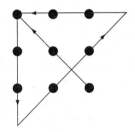

In this case, even after subjects were told to think about lines extending outside the box, still just a minority solved the problem. In effect the problem has to be restructured, or redefined, before the insight comes. The insight then seems to come very quickly. My answer to the 'count the squares' problem in Chapter 5 was 30. There is the big square itself, 9 squares made up of 4 small ones (don't forget the one in the middle), 4 squares made up of 9 small squares, and the 16 small ones themselves. Can you find any more? The left-brain skill is adding them all up.

Arousal and 'alpha'

We have seen the effect of a person's state on creativity and the role of 'downtime' and the alpha brainwave frequency. This has featured a lot in scientific research.

A person's level of arousal has been found experimentally to affect creativity. In this case, noise, at varying levels, has been used as the variable. Arousal affects scores on divergent thinking tests, but mainly at moderate levels. High arousal (typically based on sound volume) did not produce more creativity. This fits with many other experiments that seem to suggest that moderation is the rule rather than the exception in creativity. The same applies to the amount of information given, the level of rewards, etc.

In some studies EEG measurements of cortical arousal were used. This was equated to brain alpha wave generation, which has been used elsewhere as a demonstration of biofeedback. Subjects with high divergent thinking scores were able to exercise control more quickly, while the lower-scoring subjects took longer to learn and control their state through biofeedback. High-scoring subjects were also better at alpha suppression – in effect self-arousal. This seems to indicate a better sensitivity to and control over their internal state.

State control is a major component of emotional intelligence, but also a characteristic of creative people in particular. Creative persons, for example, are better able to maintain focus. This may be due to their ability to enter different states as appropriate – for example, high-frequency for conscious, analytical tasks, and low-frequency alpha for tasks requiring fluidity and originality. Creative people are also known to be open to subliminal impressions and are sensitive in other ways.

Another study compared results in poem composition in different states of attention, manipulated by noise. The noise was either predictable (as in rhythmic music) or unpredictable (as in irregular bits of sound). It was also either intelligible or unintelligible. Noise seemed to inhibit creativity, specifically in terms of breadth of attention, and this was especially so with unpredictable and unintelligible noise. These latter inhibitions were particularly marked for subjects who had a wide attention capacity and the ability for parallel processing – both traits known to be useful in writing poems, and as creative characteristics generally.

Creative stages

Experimental research has shown the importance of different stages in the creative process. One experimental task was to think of a story plot and then to write it out. It was hypothesized that the plot formulation would equate to the inspirational stage, and that the writing would equate to the elaboration stage. The results showed that creative subjects operated at a low level of arousal during the inspiration stage, recording higher alpha than the less creative subjects. Alpha state, and relaxation generally, has been strongly associated with inspiration, originality and creative flow states.

Creativity has also been associated with remote ideas, that is, ideas that come at the end of a search involving a chain of associations. Experiments have shown that the capacity for broad attention helps this process, allowing more remote associations to be found (fluidity). Arousal, as in the experiments referred to above, can induce this broadening of attention, and thus affect divergent thinking. However, the capacity for broad attention has been viewed as a longer-term trait in the nature of a personality characteristic, rather than a temporary state induced by the task or the environment. In particular, a person's intrinsic motivation to do the task, whether in a 'laboratory' or in the real world, is thought to have an even greater effect on divergent thinking and creativity generally.

Like broad attention, as we saw in Chapter 10, intrinsic motivation has been linked both to the creative process and to the personality of the creative person. It turns up as much in post hoc studies, such as of eminent historical creative people, as in experimental study.

Outside inhibitors

Some experiments considered the effects of two variables, coaction and surveillance, on creative work (coaction simply refers to the presence of other people). Both affected the state of subjects and their perceptions. The expectation of evaluation, for instance (work, it was informed, would be judged later), reduced the originality of the work, but not the technical quality of the creative products (in this case poetry and a collage). The subjects were generally dissatisfied with their work, and this is normally indicative of low intrinsic motivation and lack of pleasure in the task for its own sake. Creative subjects are usually motivated to achieve their own personal standards rather than externally set yardsticks. In this case, the *expectation* of measurement was enough to have a detrimental effect, as was the *expectation* that others (a group, indicated by the layout of chairs) would take part in the process. No work was actually examined and no audience was present. Once again the 'lone' characteristics of the creative person were confirmed.

Other experiments measured the effect of extrinsic factors on children's creative production. In one case, the evaluation was both by computer and by humans. Both, it was found, inhibited creativity. So the problem may not be a 'people' problem but rather the distraction from the job in hand and the feeling of not being in control. In this case both rewards and evaluation had a similarly detrimental effect, but less so on the younger children in the group, who may have been naturally less inhibited. The latter suggests that any kind of inhibition – not just rewards and evaluation – will tend to reduce creativity.

In similar studies undergraduates who worked on a computer were found to be less inhibited by evaluation manipulation than those who did not. The characteristics of the creative products that were most affected by evaluation were designs described by judges as 'organic' and 'well-crafted', as compared with 'logical' and 'of value'. Judgements on the latter dimension, usually considered left-brain or non-creative characteristics, were not affected significantly by the evaluation. Once again, the effect of extrinsic motivation seemed to affect the divergent thinking (especially fluidity and originality) aspects of what might be considered the whole creative process.

Replication and the real world

Compared with traditional scientific research, replication of experimental findings is rare in creativity studies. The nearest is the frequent extension of a study to include some other variable and this continues over decades. Likewise, studies may be extended to a different population, such as from children to managers, or from military personnel to undergraduates. In one sense this scientific scarcity is to be expected, insofar as creativity involves originality and novelty, and by most definitions these cannot be translated into routine, predictable behaviour. That is a dilemma to which no answers have yet been found. It partly explains the quasi-experimental scientific status of even the most carefully designed creativity experiments.

Problems and opportunities

Most experimentation seems to use a problem-solving setting, and a problem is assumed even though it may not have a single, correct answer. However, in some creative modes a problem as such is not present. We referred earlier to the creativity in problem defining, rather than problem solution. Similarly, a brainstorming approach can be just as effective in creating opportunities within a broad area of focus without having any problem as such to solve. Once again, the limitations in the experimentation seem more related to the difficulties of carrying out controlled, measurable studies in this elusive area of the human mind, rather than a misunderstanding of what creativity is about. Problem solving may need little or no creativity, and even *creative* problem solving calls upon divergent thinking for only part of an overall process. Some creative tasks like giving a piano recital may require no problem solving at all – that was part of the 'preparation'. So a heavy overemphasis on problem solving in the context of a dearth of true creativity experimental research is at best wasteful. It may just perpetuate the diversity of approaches to tackling the big creativity questions.

Another glaring absence in experimental creativity research is the use as subjects of eminently creative people, as is the case in archival or historiometric studies. These represent unambiguous examples of creativity, whereas the creative subjects normally used in experiments are based on standard creativity psychometric test scores. We cannot be sure the people we choose are really creative. But even though eminently creative people are unambiguously creative, we still do not have consensus as to what creativity is. We are only certain that it is a 'good thing', although extremely complex.

Experimental studies rely much on expert judges, especially in open-ended divergent tasks, and this is another control issue. In some cases judges are given precise guidelines as to measurement criteria, while in other cases they are allowed latitude. The latter approach tends to result in more *consistent* judging, as the person applies their own values, derived from long experience. However, the former achieves better control over experiments, and comes closer to acceptable scientific method.

These various deficiencies are bound to throw doubt on the validity of what relatively little experimental research has been carried out. Sceptically, any creativity measured in the laboratory is just 'laboratory' creativity. It cannot be equated with creativity in its varied contexts in the lives of unique individuals – much as IQ is sceptically seen to be an artificial psychometric sort of intelligence rather than the real thing.

Operant research

Some experimental studies are based on overt behaviour or actual 'operations' (operant research) rather than through psychometric instruments. These are generally confined to a limited range of indicators such as novelty, which can be reliably measured as a statistical probability, and it has also been a good measure of originality. Work has been done with dolphins in which reinforcement produced increasingly novel behaviour. Similar work was done with pigeons that were trained to do several tasks. Subsequently they were able to combine some or all of these into a novel, spontaneous sequence that integrated the responses they had learnt. This does not tell us how the spontaneous integration happened, of course, but such apparent cognition is much like the human associative process that results in a leap of understanding. Presumably a multitude of cultural and other factors do not cloud the animal experiments and the lower complexity helps us to learn something about what might otherwise seem like a mental black hole. Operant research involves 'real' behaviour rather than the 'pretend' behaviour in most creativity experiments.

Reinforcing creativity

Human experiments usually concentrate on reinforcement, or rewards, selectively given for novel behaviour. The 'reinforcers' may be linked to the amount of practice and also the instructions given, as in some of the earlier experiments described. Some experiments are of the 'list all possible uses' type, and were designed so that they would gauge fluidity, flexibility, originality and elaboration – that is, different indices of creativity. Results improved with reinforcement, but especially in the elaboration part of the process, and least in the originality aspects of the behaviour. These studies also reaffirmed the efficacy of instruction and information in fostering creativity.

An operant study involved two children and was also concerned with the effect of reinforcement (some form of reward or incentive) on divergent thinking behaviour. These experiments involved painting and block building. Reinforcement was shown to lead to increased diversity of forms in both painting and block building. An important aspect of this particular research was that the improvement in the painting task was transferred, or generalized, to the block building without additional reinforcement. That is a small start, but significant, as generalization is one of the biggest deficiencies of experimental work on creativity.

Other experiments have been done using Lego block building and felt pen drawing. These results further supported the generalizability, and also the durability of changes in creative behaviour resulting from various reinforcement interventions. Given the present great interest in fostering creativity in children, the work has obvious implications for the classroom. The findings also validate a 'reinforcement' training approach to creativity, such as in business.

Operant research in controlled conditions, although sparse and limited in its scope, is significant for creativity research generally. In some cases a cause and effect relationship can be established – such as between the independent variable of reinforcement and the dependent variable of novel behaviour – rather than simple correlation. Usually, causality is neither designed into the research nor claimed – hence, again, 'quasi-science'.

As we have seen, operant research attempts to show the generalizability of results, or their transferability to more normal outside conditions. This is important for training programmes that companies hope will reflect in performance back in the workplace. Some of the technology for this sort of study was based on trying to ensure that clinical interventions would be maintained back in the patient's own environment. In the case of the above creativity experiments with children, the parallel is to show that they are generalizable, say, to education. Findings based on both psychometric and operant research form a sound basis for developing personal creativity.

Summary of experimental findings

Experimental studies in creativity add to our understanding over and above the other approaches we have considered, in various ways:

■ Information in the form of instruction, procedural guidance and 'reinforcement' can manipulate creativity in open-ended tasks and produce divergent thinking. But beyond a certain level, more information does not necessarily mean more creativity. It seems that above a threshold, further information is of no benefit, and this 'in moderation' factor applies to other interventions also.

■ Imagery can be manipulated to increase inventiveness.

■ Intuition manifests itself reliably as a characteristic of creative people, and the 'intuitive leap' can be demonstrated. Likewise, creative people are sensitive to subliminal cues.

■ Creative people tend to be able to control alpha brain state and respond to biofeedback methods.

■ Creative thinking is associated with a broad attentional capacity, which can be enhanced by arousal.

■ Attitudes affect creative production and are relatively easy to manipulate in experimental conditions. This forms an important area of focus for increasing personal creativity.

■ Intrinsic motivation and interest in the task for its own sake has been conclusively associated with novel thinking and behaviour.

■ Emotion (affect) has an effect on creative problem solving, but positive effects are lost above a certain level ('moderation in all things creative'; interventions are optimal rather than maximal).

■ Different kinds of problems elicit different degrees and characteristics of creativity so experimental results may not be generalizable.

As it happens, few intelligent people need to draw upon scientific experiments to be convinced of the importance of creativity, and few question its main characteristics of fluidity and originality of thinking. Indeed, compared with the period before

Guilford's address in 1950, and the wilderness years of behaviourism, we have come a long way. In particular, although as yet undefined, creativity has been more or less *demystified*, along with the Cartesian idea of mind. But the findings can help us to understand creativity in our own lives and how we can practically increase and apply it. The scientific conclusions also help remove some of the connotations of madness and eccentricity – we have less chance of getting locked up.

From this overview of scientific research the trend – seen with a little optimism – is towards integration of the various approaches to the study of creativity, rather than the compartmentalizing tendency of the past. Meanwhile, its importance and complexity, as almost universally acknowledged, continue to grow the deeper we delve. Its amenability to interventions and different kinds of training is also well accepted, more from the experimental work described in this chapter than from psychometric research. So, whatever creativity is – and we mostly know it when we see it or feel it – you can have more of it in your life.

13

Creativity in business

Creativity is personal. It cannot be written into the memorandum and articles of a company nor embodied into a corporate legal entity of any kind. Its habitat is no less than a human brain. A creative business, if such is not a contradiction in terms, can only be creative by virtue of its people. It is only through its people that it can do *anything*, of course, but harnessing personal creativity is a particularly special case. Even a household-name corporate brand will lose its value in a few months with the wrong people at the helm or if their creativity dries up. Conversely, a creative leader or key player can transform a business. The rest of the book has addressed individual creativity. Creative people working in an organization have special problems and may face important decisions. Managers, likewise, need freedom to be creative and to get the best out of their staff. The job of the corporation is somehow to harness that individual creativity and translate it into corporate goals.

Bureaucratization

Business wants to act creatively, or at least to produce creative products, however it does it. But we need to approach the subject of creativity in business from a very different perspective as compared to individual creativity. A company is a legal entity that:

- doesn't get brainwaves;
- doesn't have insight;
- is devoid of imagination;
- doesn't 'incubate' problems;
- doesn't wake in the night with an answer;
- never has intuition;
- is without feeling;
- doesn't care.

An organization has sometimes been compared to the left side of the human brain, rather than the creative right side. But that is too flattering to the business. When you turn the lights out and lock the doors an organization stops doing anything, including thinking, if it ever thought. It is no more wise the next morning.

That's the relatively good news. The bad news is that an organization tends to gravitate towards a bureaucratic, singularly non-creative method of working if left to its own devices for more than a week. It stifles personal creativity, originality, risk taking, and just about any characteristic that might help its people to be creative. All this is without trying, and simply in the nature of something inanimate not designed or equipped for that purpose. The organizational fate is as sure as aches and pains then death in humans. Bureaucracy is inevitable. The task is to delay its onset (such as by continual decentralization) and introduce counter-forces – like creative people. A creative CEO, for instance, will help to create the right culture and will understand the needs of creative people.

We can make do without creativity, as most organizations do anyway, although they hardly realize it, and if they did they would be loath to admit it now that creativity is in vogue. This is a popular course, if by default rather than design. A lot of businesses live a long time on *past* creativity – even a single, revolutionary product or service idea. A profitable edge can be maintained through economies of scale and efficiency in what is an imperfect and brand-loyal market. However, when creativity dries up, failure is just a matter of time.

Alternatively, an organization can glean its creativity from its people, who in the main vent their creative tendencies on out-of-work creative pursuits, and have plenty of spare creative capacity. The possibility is that some crumbs from the weekend table of creativity will reach the office on Monday mornings. But there is no guarantee that this option will work. Staff know only too well the risks of suggesting anything out of the ordinary that might upset an immediate boss and probably never reach higher management – so why bother? It means swimming against the corporate tide.

Debureaucratization

An option is to make the best of a bad job and try to mitigate the detrimental effects of the organization on the creativity of its people, which entails making the organization less of a negative influence on the personal creativity of its people, with the strategic but rearguard goal of debureaucratization. Tactically it involves carrots and sticks, with endemic staff problems and fire-fighting. It boils down to making the environment amenable to whatever turns on personal creativity, such as:

- freedom from bureaucratic constraints;
- autonomy;
- a good supply of challenging projects;
- choice;
- management support;
- a relaxing physical environment;
- no time pressures;
- rewards for risk taking and innovation;
- applauding originality;
- turning a blind eye to rules;
- allowing some fun.

The search for corporate creativity is a tall proposition and the individual creative dream may become a corporate nightmare.

It is no surprise that far fewer examples of creative organizations come to mind than creative people. With the exception of entrepreneurs, creative people mostly come from the worlds of science and art rather than business management. Furthermore, where innovative companies do get noticed, a creative CEO or R&D team is usually cited in the same breath and it is usually all too clear where the real credit should lie. The company will resort to whatever structures and devices might harness individual creativity and counter organizational inertia. It becomes clear that the organization reached the rare status of creativity *despite* its natural bureaucratic tendencies. It came from individuals who happened to have the freedom and power within the organization to exercise their creativity.

Sometimes the degree of freedom given to key workers makes them in effect freelance contractors. Some companies go the whole way and formalize the separation. Whole creative functions are contracted out along with cleaning and payroll. This is to avoid the envy of staff in more mundane roles, and ensure the removal of organizational fetters.

Creative cultures

Smaller organizations present less of a problem, however, hence the tendency to decentralize and break up larger structures. In a small organization a particularly creative team, especially at board level, can create a culture that spreads right through the firm. Although it does not manufacture creative people (creative people spend little time on training others to be creative), it can engender a spirit of excitement, innovation, risk, anarchy and the sort of cultural traits that help rather than hinder creativity. But quasi-left brain, cold rationale renders such a fire-in-the-belly commitment the exception rather than the rule, and its influence increases with the size of the organization. Hierarchical growth, specialization, standard employee incentives, the need for financial control and short-term pressures from shareholders all combine to create a cost-effective, efficient, profitable bureaucracy that is going nowhere. The organization overwhelms individual creativity and scares off risky ideas. If profitable growth is the goal, failure is inevitable in due course.

It all seems like a high price to pay, so a business has to decide whether creativity is a gain or a drain – whether it is worth all the trouble. The question has been well addressed by business umbrella organizations, professional institutes and government bodies. One very large study in a commercially available report put the 'gain' votes at 90 per cent and the 'drain' at 10 per cent. So businesses overwhelmingly see creativity as *a good thing* – or say they do. Most say they encourage creativity. Some describe systems and facilities that specifically promote it. However, studies of actual creativity, based on creative products, tell a different story. They largely bear out the negative effect of hierarchical organizations (which almost all are) on innovation described above.

Towards corporate creativity

Corporate creativity takes one of four broad approaches. Understanding these can help the individual creative employee as well as enlightened management. For a highly creative person it may mean an important career decision.

1. Separation

The first approach can go to the extreme of physical separation of the creative part of the company, whatever the formal hierarchical relationship. Most likely a compromise solution will be reached, resulting in at least a different *culture* within the larger corporate culture, and this will minimize the negative influences on creativity.

Most companies follow competitors, such as in R&D spend, or otherwise follow what they understand to be 'best practice'. However, no two companies are alike and transplanting creativity systems and structures is no more likely to reproduce the results obtained elsewhere than trying to transplant the elusive

characteristics of corporate 'excellence'. Such standard characteristics are likely to be rejected by the 'foreign' corporate body
with its own distinctive culture. The so-called 'excellent
company' is not immune: 'best practice' characteristics may not
work for long as the world changes around it.

True creativity is unique and not amenable to replicable
formulae, so this is one part of the business that will not
respond to standard systems, proven formulae, or somebody
else's 'best practice'. However, removing or annoying free
thinkers may be nails in the coffin for the company. Creativity is
a scarce resource in *every* part of a business, not just those parts
traditionally thought of that way, such as research and development. For example, you need creativity to control costs and
streamline operations as much as to conceive of new products.
It all affects the same bottom line.

2. Fostering personal creativity

A better approach is to start from the creative person's perspective – get into their shoes. We have a good idea of the sort of
environment that supports creativity, and the characteristics of
creative people that we need to encourage and foster that we
listed earlier. These form the foundation for change when
looking at creativity from the point of view of the creative
person. The typical creative process (Chapter 5) confirms these,
as do the characteristics of known creative people (Chapter 4).
They provide the benchmark of conditions a company has to
strive to meet.

How these needs are translated into an organization will vary
from case to case, and some needs are more difficult to respond
to than others. For example, creativity includes an incubation
stage and that means time – in fact an unspecified period of
time. It often means long periods of concentration and abandonment of all routine. Office routines and hours may be
turned upside down. The term 'flexible working' as applied
elsewhere in the company would be no more than a euphemism.
Fellow workers may question whether such conditions mean

'work' at all. Conventional supervision may not fit the culture, and an extraordinary level of trust has to exist. It might preclude team working for periods as this limits individual freedom and attention. Any hierarchy would need to be so flat as to have little meaning, and even a paper organization structure will be part of the 'perceived control', and 'rules' that are detrimental to creativity. At best, creative modes of working will be viewed with envy or scepticism by less well-treated employees. Local autonomy, far from unloading the creative 'function', is sure to mean time and effort in the overall management of the company.

Company considerations

An organization will need to consider each of the above creative traits separately, and allow for the many variables in the particular company. These include:

- the creative people;
- the kind of product or service, especially 'creative products' (what the company expects from its creative people);
- the physical environment (such as relaxing accommodation or a pleasant location);
- the corporate culture;
- the leader and his or her style.

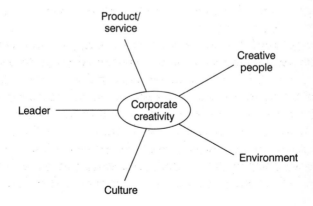

Each solution will be at best a compromise, but will invariably be better than an imposed system or structure from outside. Most importantly, the creative brains of the people themselves should be brought to bear on the problem. This offers real benefits:

■ It ensures 'ownership' of final arrangements – a fundamental requirement of the planning process and staff commitment.
■ It will probably result in the most practical and possibly ingenious solutions. Creative people start by asking the right questions. They know their own needs best.
■ It incorporates the concerns and perceptions of the people themselves rather than what management *thinks* these are, and thus stands a better chance of success.
■ It takes the most direct communication route, thus avoiding the number one problem of poor communication.

This organic process may stimulate bigger changes than are first anticipated, possibly at a corporate level such as in product and market strategy. What might otherwise be seen as 'people problems' may turn into strategic opportunities – another role for the creative mind. Insofar as the future of any business lies in the creative minds of a small percentage of its people, they should be part of the strategic policy-making process anyway. All the creative resources and techniques of a company should be focused on this vital job of creating and maintaining a culture of creativity throughout the organization. In customer service, for example, creativity means staying one step ahead of the customer, anticipating rather than reacting to their needs.

3. Training and techniques

Techniques to achieve creativity goals are readily available in their scores. But these must be seen as secondary to creative *people* and a *culture* that supports them. Techniques can be utilized as part of ongoing creativity training, and many techniques are known to be effective with staff generally who do not occupy 'creative' posts or carry out 'creative' functions. Creativity training, as well as creativity, has got a thumbs-up from contemporary businesses. Although the return on investment of such training is not easily measured, a creative *culture* and environment can only add benefit in any cost–benefit analysis, just as a culture of customer service will enhance corporate marketing. The nature and measurement of creative training is wide open for debate, but it is certain that no part of an organization (including the training department) can fail to benefit from a dose of creative thinking.

Creativity techniques are easier to incorporate into the company's training and ongoing processes than making cultural or attitudinal changes. This is partly for the wrong reason, in that many techniques use left-brain as well as right-brain concepts and do not address the crucial creative parts of the total creative process. Such training methods happen as easily as bureaucracy. So, whilst techniques may have less effect than a well-motivated creative person – who doesn't need techniques, or designs his or her own – they are more amenable to decentralized use, less risky and more predictable. Some very large corporations carry out creativity training for all or the majority of their staff.

There remains the choice of techniques and mode of delivery, which is almost endless. Unfortunately, the techniques that produce the most potentially creative products require the most creativity, or 'right-brain thinking skills', on the part of the people using them. They are no more than 'provocative' tools that help to stimulate the innate creativity that is there to start with. As a training investment, therefore, there is more mileage to be got from techniques that train for *creativity* (such as relaxation and visualization) than from those applicable to doing specific tasks or solving known problems. (This is amplified in the following chapter.)

4. Cultural sheep dip

Another approach is to subject all staff to creativity 'conditioning', in the same way that customer service attitude changing is approached. The philosophy here is that every person in the company should be creative in their work, and customers, staff and shareholders alike stand to benefit. Sadly, this approach will usually have even less success than customer care 'sheep dips', mainly because creativity is not amenable to conventional instruction and training, just as it does not fit well into scientific research methods. The flow experience can occur in every role, and creative insight can happen in the most unexpected of contexts. We generally lose out by stereotyping creativity and creative people.

An effective approach is to identify staff whose creative thinking is most critical to the company and seek to make their environment amenable to creativity. This will reflect the known characteristics of creative people and the creative processes that we covered in earlier chapters. In summary, creativity in business does not consist in creating a creative function – like a marketing department – but in fostering and harnessing creativity in individual people. This may require elements from all four of the above approaches, but will depend on the unique culture of the company and the extent to which that – in addition to structure and systems – needs to be changed. If so, it starts at the top.

14

CQ booster programme

Human creativity does not lend itself to experimental science and belongs with one of the softest of the soft sciences. Like intelligence, it cannot be satisfactorily defined, or measured quantitatively. IQ puts numerical measurements on certain aspects of intelligence but does not address creativity, or indeed other aspects or kinds of intelligence, such as are included in EQ (emotional intelligence or quotient) and 'multiple intelligences'. Although numerical 'scores' have been applied to EQ, these are not standardized so have little meaning beyond individual proprietary psychometric tests.

What's in a CQ?

The term CQ is also subjective and less amenable to even qualitative measurements because of its spontaneous characteristics. But we know creativity when we see it. We all have it – however long it has lain underused. And as we have seen, we can all increase it personally by a large factor. We can therefore use the shorthand term CQ as including all the main features of creativity we have covered in the book, without pretending that one or all of these features can be translated into a number or absolute 'score'. CQ can also include creative products, of the sort we covered in Chapter 6. You can identify what 'products' apply to the creativity you aspire to personally.

CQ also bears the influence of the 'systems' in which your creativity operates – such as at work, in a sport or via the wider culture. By taking account of all the individual factors comprised in the CQ description you can therefore be sure that you are monitoring the 'real thing'. With such awareness you will have little doubt how your personal quotient fares – whether in quality or in quantity – over a period.

The 'wow' factor

This is not to say that you cannot measure more specifically or quantitatively in different areas of creativity. For instance, you can measure fluidity, flexibility and originality – divergent thinking components – as the popular creativity tests do. By keeping a creativity journal you can also monitor components of your CQ that could not be measured psychometrically because they occur spontaneously. For example, you can record insights, or 'ideas out of the blue', and rate them for quality at one to five stars or a score out of 10. The same applies to 'flow' experiences. These will have a quantitative time period, and a place or context, as well as a star rating or 'wow' factor.

DIY CQ

By doing your own CQ monitoring you will learn what stimulates different creative events and processes and how to turn them on more consciously. Put another way, in understanding and seeking to *measure* your creativity you will *improve* it in the process. If you can say you have doubled your CQ, based on your own round-the-clock measurement, you have done more than the best psychometric instruments can do. That is as it should be. It is *your* creativity and *you* decide on the products to aim for. You will *know* what is true creativity and what is not, and the different quality and usefulness of creative thoughts. Your creativity is unique.

You can in any event be more sure of your creative productivity than you could ever be based on an incomplete psychometric test of questionable validity, however popular. You can boost your CQ to whatever level you can realistically imagine and be a better all-round person for it.

Triple booster programme

You can exercise and improve your creativity on a day-to-day basis and we will concentrate on this in this final chapter. Consider this a personal programme for boosting your CQ. It is not a system or formula but a round-the-clock way of thinking and lifestyle. You create the attitudes and beliefs upon which your creativity is based. Because it is so all-embracing, I have made sure it is easy and pleasurable. If any parts aren't, don't do them. But you may be curious to know how you will feel once you have given them a try.

It's a triple booster because there are three general approaches which you can adopt in parallel, which we will cover first:

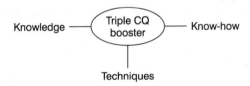

Knowledge

This is about *understanding your creativity*, which much of the book has been about. For example, we have asked the questions:

- ■ What is creativity?
- ■ What are the traits of creative people?
- ■ What thinking processes do they use?

■ What are the sorts of products that creative people produce?

You can check back on these three main topics in Chapters 4 to 6 in particular, but they recur throughout the book. 'Knowledge' includes information about your brain, its capacity and some of the special ways in which it operates to produce quality thinking (Chapter 3). It also includes the background information in the introduction and early chapters. All this creates motivation sufficient to get you on the path to serious creative thinking.

Knowing what your brain is capable of achieving is great for your creativity self-belief and general confidence. You may want to improve your true intelligence also, and we showed how intelligence relates to creativity in Chapter 7. As it happens, you can't help becoming more intelligent (in its broader senses, not just IQ) as you become more creative. We saw that high creativity is correlated to average or above-average IQ and you can approach these from both directions. *Boost Your Intelligence* (Kogan Page) takes it from the intelligence point of view, including boosting your IQ.

Creativity also includes the role of culture and other 'systemic' or environmental influences on your creativity (Chapters 8 and 9), the state of research and the main findings from the literature (Chapters 11 and 12). It includes its application in business (Chapter 13) (for those who need to be creative inside an organization). Finally, you need to understand the role and nature of motivation in your creative life as we saw in Chapter 10, and this is also covered in the chapters on psychometrics and experimental research.

Know-how and conditioning

The second approach concerns the skills you can apply based on your ever-deepening knowledge of creativity, and especially your own creativity as you come to notice and reflect on it. For example, we saw from the experimental and psychometric research the part that information, conditions and rewards play in a person's creative output. You can put these other factors into practice to affect your CQ directly. For example, based on your knowledge of the research findings, you can plan specific 'rewards' for yourself that will enhance rather than quash your creativity. The difference, as we learnt, can be subtle and wrongly perceived rewards can be counterproductive.

Similarly, you can explore a subject or project you want to become involved in more deeply in order to reach the critical level of intrinsic motivation that you will need to create something worthwhile. You can also draw on your own resources and motivation from other parts of your life memory store. All this concerns *doing* – but *specific*, *purposeful* doing based on up-to-date information on the different aspects of creativity we have covered throughout the book.

Foundation skills

Know-how also takes the form of foundational skills such as relaxing and inducing alpha state that help creative thinking and 'flow'. This basic self-conditioning needs to be: 1) a *skill*, which needs application and practice like any skill, and 2) a *habit*, so that you don't have to *try* or consciously think about being creative.

As we saw, your self-belief as a 'creative person' will affect your creativity in a fundamental way. Therefore know-how about changing your beliefs where necessary gives a lot of leverage. It is worth a dozen techniques. Attitude and emotion also affect creative performance in a big way and these need 'state control' know-how, and proper understanding of your *self* (more knowledge, but *self*-knowledge). Self-knowledge, or intrapersonal intelligence, will take you a long way to aligning your *state* as well as your beliefs for optimal creativity. Some creative tasks seem to depend entirely on the mood we are in.

Task-related techniques

The third approach is to have both knowledge and know-how in the various techniques you can apply to actual creative projects, tasks or situations. Most creativity techniques can be described as 'provocative', in that they provoke divergent thinking, multiple possibilities and different viewpoints. These techniques, without the high-leverage 'conditioning' of the second approach, will do little for your creativity *as a long-term trait*. They can, however, be effective on a task-by-task basis, and more so as you get to use them intuitively. But techniques work far better given the *mind* of a creative person. The above conditioning approach also involves techniques, such as relaxation and visualization, but these apply to you as a *person* rather than to the tasks you are doing.

All techniques involve some measure of skill, which means they work better the more you use them. Most – like brainstorming – demand a degree of divergent thinking anyway so are of little use without innate creativity. That is why techniques on their own are of little use to some people. Several different techniques do more or less the same job, so you can choose the ones that work best for you. There are scores of techniques – some with whole books covering them – so there is only space here for a selection. I have described these as main *types* of technique, as there are variations on any theme, and any 'family' of techniques provokes the same creative tendencies. These techniques are mostly in the public domain and you can get information about them from the Internet or in your local library.

Self-conditioning skills

You have already covered the 'knowledge' approach by reading the book, and you can refer back as you wish. The rest of this chapter covers know-how in the three key areas of creative self-belief, creative state, and lifestyle, and then a description of the main kinds of techniques.

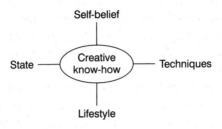

Self-belief

Self-belief means what you believe about yourself, in this case in the areas of your life associated with creativity. A single negative self-belief like 'I'm not an ideas person' or 'I'm not musical' can make increasing your CQ an unnecessarily uphill struggle. Conversely, a person who believes they are creative will invariably show it in their creative products and achievements. Self-belief is powerful and self-fulfilling and underlies all our behaviour. Most self-beliefs date back many years and are long past their sell-by date in reflecting what we are today. Even though negative beliefs may have affected your behaviour, because of their self-fulfilling nature, they need not affect your present potential. This is where the information you have gained throughout the book will help. For example, information about your innate creative functions and enormous brain capacity, and mental patterns, will gradually change your belief about your own creativity and become reality. This replaces past perceptions based on out-of-place comments from well-meaning parents and teachers and incomplete information.

Belief affirmation

Creativity is a typical self-belief and changing it is straightforward and painless. The first stage is to identify each present belief impinging on your creativity and check that it stacks up with your present *goals and values*. If not, you can change it and believe what you want. Simply reverse it, or make it more specific, for example 'I enjoy challenges and come up with more and more ingenious solutions'. Say this and write it down. Your unconscious mind requires repetition and it is better to overdo it than not get your new message across. Treat it like writing out lines at school, but this time experience the pleasure and confident state as you start to believe what you say and write.

Acting it out

Next align your behaviour with your belief. That means acting it out. If you keep winning races you have to believe, sooner or later, that you are a winner of races, whatever beliefs you harbour from childhood. You have plenty of choice as to doing creative things, even extending to fun exercises you can download from the Internet. Likewise, by changing your routines so that you see new things and different perspectives you will start to think and act more creatively. Your belief will fall into line, now that you have expressed it openly. Behaviour is *evidence* of your belief, so play the create part.

Just imagine

If your behaviour cannot stretch to anything creative, you have other choices. Simply vividly *imagine* yourself being creative – in whatever areas you had in mind when you made your new belief. Realistic visualization does the same job as experience but without the risk of failure (which is not the evidence you need for your new self-image). Once again, repetition is the secret. The realism comes with practice. Just do what you do when you dream about a holiday, a new car or whatever you dream about. *Act out* whatever you decide you believe, both inside, by multi-sensory visualization, and outside, in the real world. In the real world choose low-risk tasks in which you will clock up repeated successes. Inside you can aim as high as you like, but make sure you always come out on top.

Imagine being creative *in different contexts*, such as in specific work and social roles as well as, say, in your hobby – in which you are probably already creative. That way, you will not leave part of your life untouched, as that may be the very prop your old belief needs to sustain itself ('I told you you couldn't hold a note'). The more examples of creative behaviour you mentally enact, the more your unconscious mind will have to toe the line and start supporting your new belief. Once the mental habit is changed, you are on a virtuous self-fulfilling cycle of creative thinking and attitude.

There are several specific belief-change techniques you can borrow from neuro-linguistic programming and some of my other books include these. However, you will have no trouble aligning your creativity self-image with the information you have already gained about creativity, and simple skills like relaxing and visualizing which always respond to application and practice.

These techniques apply also to your attitude or frame of mind – in other words, any longer-term thinking patterns that may affect your shorter-term state and behaviour. Treat them as habits. To correct a bad driving habit you just change whatever you do for about three weeks. At first you always have to think about it, but then your lapses get fewer and fewer until you suddenly realize that you are behaving the new way without thinking about it.

Belief is a mega factor in personal creativity. That means that any change will ripple through to a disproportionate increase in final creative products. By starting at the beliefs end you gain leverage. By simply using techniques you may relieve surface symptoms but your negative, *disempowering* belief will win out in the end. So you need a creative shot in the arm for every task or problem you face. By changing your belief you will act out your creativity without trying.

State control

State of mind is ephemeral and does not play the fairly predicable part that a deep-seated belief or value plays. However, it still gives you leverage. When you are in the right state of mind things seem to go well without techniques and systems, and when you use them techniques work better. It doesn't work the other way round and external techniques do not produce spin-off mental patterns that internal changes do.

We are most concerned here with a state that is conducive to creative thinking. As we have seen, this is typically a relaxed, 'unbusy' state of mind associated neurophysiologically with slow, alpha brainwaves. It reflects the 'downtime' end of the uptime–downtime continuum, and 'soft' rather than 'hard focus'. Inducing the state is easier for some people than others, but anyone can develop the skill with practice.

Just relax

The mind and body are one system and state control starts with physical relaxation. There are plenty of systems for relaxing and it depends on whether you want a quick fix for a specific situation, such as when summoned by the boss, or as part of a more ordered, purposeful conditioning programme. The latter comes first, then you can 'anchor' the state to be used at short notice. With about 20 minutes of uninterrupted time you can really go 'downtime' and enjoy clear imagery as well as physical relaxation which is good for your health and well-being.

A popular method is to progressively think about each limb, imagining it to be heavy or light or separate from your body. Accompany this with slow, deep breathing which even on its own is a sure relaxer. Start with limbs away from your head and move upwards, concentrating especially on your neck, face and eyes. 'Busy' thoughts may invade your mind but simply switch your thoughts back to your body and the pleasant, sensory experience that comes with complete relaxation. As you become fully relaxed you can start on your mental state, and this is best done by visualization. Experience a pleasant, safe place where everyday thoughts are left behind and you can experience your inner reality. Explore your special place in sights, sounds and feelings, and tune them up to perfection to arrive at inner as well as outer calm.

You can accompany mental relaxation, or alpha inducement, with counting down if you like. That way you will come to associate descending numbers with progressive physical and mental relaxation and it will happen more and more easily in the future. You will need fewer and fewer numbers once you get some practice – say 10 down to 1. Leave the final numbers – 3, 2, 1 – to associate with final *mental* clarity and the vivid imagery that tells you that you are ready to do mental business.

This is a trance-like state that is conducive to suggestion and all manner of internal manipulation such as recalling memories, creating a future through visualizing it, and making the belief changes as we have just discussed. When you reach the state you want, anchor it kinaesthetically, such as by a finger-touching-thumb circle, or any simple movement or gesture that you would never normally use. Check out your anchor later and again the following morning to ensure that it brings you instantly to the downtime state you want to recall. The advantage of these techniques is that they work for anybody, whatever your disposition, even if it takes a few more 'runs'.

Recall this positive state whenever you face a problem or situation in which you wish to be calm, focused, perceptive and creative. It works wonders for high blood pressure and stress, and will instantly rescue you from less helpful states that take you unawares. Get into this state when you want to install new beliefs by mentally experiencing your behaviour in different situations.

You can also anchor specific creative states from memory. These empowering memories will typically be in parts of your life in which you tend to be more confident and creative. The aim in this case is to make it available to any part of your life at any time. Re-experience the moment in which you were in 'flow' or got a great idea or ready-made solution – in other words, the state you would like to turn on more often to increase your CQ and be more productive. Anchor it just as above, test it out a few times over a period, then use it in live situations.

Lifestyle

This is a general category of self-conditioning based on day-to-day activities, routines and lifestyle. The main objective is to develop lifestyle activities and habitual behaviour that will enhance your creativity. We have seen that associative thinking draws on your existing mental database of life knowledge and experience. So the more there is inside to work on, the greater choice your unconscious mind has when doing an association trawl. This happens during a period of incubation after your conscious mind has dropped a problem, not being able to take it any further.

Pack as much knowledge and new experiences as you can into your life. You don't have to take them all up as hobbies or special interests. Even a single exposure to a new experience creates a whole new neural network that will enrich your creativity. Reading is an obvious way to do this, as your mind doesn't really differentiate between vividly imagining something and the real thing. So you can do things and go to places that might be impractical in real life. Television documentaries do a similar job, except that you use your senses less, so it doesn't produce such a realistic, memorable mental record. This is why we tend to remember certain books and radio drama, even going back years, more than television and video.

All of this you can do purposefully – in other words, just *do it* – whether you consider yourself creative or not, and it will make a positive impact on your creativity. In conjunction with the psychological conditioning we have just covered, you will multiply your creative output. That is simply a function of plentiful brain capacity and the self-fulfilling nature of belief, attitude and temperament. And this CQ boost is before ever embarking on provocative techniques, some of which are very effective.

CQ is nothing like the limited IQ concept which is concerned with certain aspects of intelligence which mirror school-type work. We are already so left-brain conditioned that there are diminishing returns for effort in improving that part of our mental processing. So you look for marginal, percentage improvement. Underutilized or atrophied creative functions, on the other hand, are just waiting to be rekindled. Moreover, IQ reflects *conscious* thinking processes which we know from the research can only handle about half a dozen variables at one time. The unconscious mind, on the other hand, comprises billions of data bits and more or less infinite potential cross-associations. That is where insights arise and that is a better reflection of your potential for increasing your CQ.

Getting out of a rut

The other approach to lifestyle conditioning is to change routines and your environment. That might mean, for example:

- changing your route to work;
- changing meal and other routines;
- moving the furniture around;
- walking rather than driving;
- driving rather than walking;
- going somewhere out of character for a holiday;
- planning to meet new people;
- joining clubs;
- resigning from clubs.

This means deliberately shuffling your brain patterns so that they become less entrenched and more amenable to cross-association. That is what creativity is all about. You can take it into your own hands, genes or no genes, and whatever the teacher told you about your artistic, musical or creative skills. Every human mind is god-like in its creative potential.

Creativity techniques

Many techniques can help to stimulate creativity and mostly are used in problem solving and to foster creativity generally in training courses. Most are designed to stimulate divergent thinking, although they are most effective when the user is already a divergent thinker. Just as positive thinkers tend to buy positive thinking books, creative thinkers are at home with creativity techniques. But with the background in this book and the conditioning skills we have just covered, anyone can get benefit from the popular techniques when applied to live work or personal problems. I have included just a sample, but even these overlap a lot, and many other similar techniques do more or less the same thing.

Chunking

Chunking involves taking a problem to a higher or lower 'logical' level. To illustrate the concept, take any word or object you can think of – say dog. Logical chunking up might go to pet (the *class* to which dogs belong, and of which dogs are an example), then on up to mammal, animal, living thing and so on. Chunking down could go to paw (as a part) or spaniel (as a type).

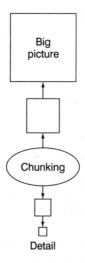

These up and down dimensions reflect the big picture as against parts, or detail in the thinking process. We have met these throughout the book and they roughly relate to the brain hemispheres. By provoking respective close-up and stand-back views (tree and forest) you can simulate what your brain does anyway.

Chunking a problem up might suggest a larger problem of which the present problem is only a symptom or part. For example, the problem of not being able to pay the gas bill might be chunked up to the problem of not living within your means, or chunked down to where specifically you might save on gas consumption.

The technique is very useful in negotiation, as chunking up tends to get agreement. We all believe in 'doing good' and 'being fair'; we all want a 'win–win' conclusion. Chunking down may isolate a minor sticking point which would not cost much to concede or provide a win–win trade-off. Specialist negotiation is an example of a practical creative thinking skill that can be quickly converted into money value. It is also an invaluable tool when dealing with children and teenagers, although this may require even more creativity.

Brainstorming

This is an old group technique and there is now some doubt about whether it is as effective as individual techniques in terms of person-hours to creative products. We discussed 'better brainstorming' in Chapter 5. It involves about half a dozen people coming up with ideas intuitively on an issue or problem. Its significance as a technique lies in the ground rules that apply. These reflect the attitude one must have at the creative as compared with the evaluative stage of a task or project:

■ Criticism is not allowed – you suspend judgement.
■ Freethinking is encouraged – even crazy ideas. One idea tends to trigger another.

◼ Quantity rather than quality is the rule. Just keep coming up with more ideas and leave the quality to be evaluated later.

◼ Be ready to add to and improve other ideas so that combinations and associations are explored.

◼ Get someone to write down ideas.

Unfortunately, however you brief the group, usually (on the old 80–20 rule) one or two of the group take up most 'air time'. As we have already seen, research has shown that coaction, or the presence of other people per se, can inhibit creativity.

Brain writing and brain sketching

Another version, brain writing – there are several versions – overcomes this by having the group first work as individuals. For example, each person writes, say, four ideas on a piece of paper concerning a problem or issue that has been stated. These are circulated and each person builds on the ideas and writes down improvements and variations, which are further elaborated on by the next person and so on. As papers are passed around this allows more even involvement. The absence of group dynamics avoids 'politics' and you can incorporate anonymity so that every idea gets proper attention. The written ideas also give a permanent record, and can be referred to at a later evaluation stage, perhaps as a group.

A variation on the brain writing theme is brain sketching, in which a drawing represents the problem rather than words, and the drawing is successively added to in order to improve and refine it. Graphical techniques probably reflect 'right brain' thinking processes more than words, and can tap creative skills that usually remain under the surface. The graphical format may restrict the kind of problem, but conversely, it can be ideal for certain kinds of problems such as product design, layouts, logistics, graphical logos and suchlike where the solution is graphical or spatial.

Flowscapes

This is one of the techniques that Edward de Bono invented and is covered fully in his books. The flowscape is based on the idea that thoughts tend to 'flow' one into another rather than come in discrete units – like the idea of word association. It suggests the question 'Where might this lead?' rather than 'What is this?'

You decide on the problem, issue or opportunity and write it down in as few words as possible. Then write down the first thing that comes into your head when thinking of the statement or idea, and so on until you cannot think of any more, so that you finish with a list of short statements.

Give these 'perceptions' a letter: A, B, C and so on. Then decide which of the other thoughts on your list naturally follows or flows from each lettered thought – where the idea might lead. The letter representing where each thought leads is added to every item on the list so that you have a 'from' and 'to' letter for each one. These you arrange graphically with an arrow going from one to the other in the direction of the 'flow' until every item is accounted for, but once only. Each letter goes to one letter only (the nearest intuitive fit) but that letter can appear more than once – in other words, several different thoughts can flow to the same one. Here is an example from an earlier book on creativity, *Train Your Brain*.

The problem. You have a faithful and loyal manager who has worked hard for you over the years. He is getting older and the work is getting too much for him. He has not yet reached retirement age and he is unwilling to take early retirement.

The letters on the right are where the thought 'flows' to.

A	Been with you many years and loyal	I
B	Does not want to retire	E
C	Need for a new person	F
D	Money is no problem	B
E	Turf and territory is a problem	B
F	Difficult to indicate inadequacy	G
G	Manager is a sensitive person	I

H	It has to happen sometime	C
I	Effect on morale elsewhere	B
J	Hints have been ignored and reflected	B

This is what the flows look like as a diagram:

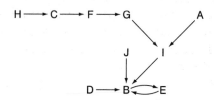

In the A thought, for example, the fact that he has been with you many years suggests an effect on morale if he were to leave. The thought flows intuitively to the morale thought more than to others. All the technique does is record your perception in graphical form to simulate the way that we think normally. You can then analyse the flowscape and, in a more logical mode, deduce further ideas and conclusions. The pattern of flow can suggest interesting conclusions and may unblock the problem. For example, using this example:

Point B This is termed a 'collector' point, because several items lead into it. The manager simply does not want to retire. To sack him would be ungrateful for his loyal services and would affect morale elsewhere.

Point I This is also a collector point which collects up some other feeders and then feeds them into B. In essence, it affirms that sacking is not an option.

Chain H–C–F–G The need for a change indicated by this 'chain' is eventually blocked by the impossibility of retiring the manager against his will.

Loop B–E This is known as a 'stable loop'. Comprising just two elements of the list, it is a very simple one. It seems the manager does not want to retire and does not want to give up his territory or turf so there is no possibility of moving him to a different position. The solution might be to promote him and to have other people working under him. This way he gets to keep the turf but the work he cannot cope with gets done by other people.

There are no wrong ideas. They are simply your thoughts and the technique helps you to get the most out of them. In fact what may seem like a silly idea may provide an important link in the chain and generate a new line of thinking. Techniques like this do not do the creative thinking for you. You have to come up with thoughts, and the more insightful they are the more you are likely to crack the problem and reach a quality solution. However, they are good for creativity practice and even on the first attempt you may be able to solve a real problem. Once you realize that you can always come up with intuitive ideas in quantity you will start to have confidence in your creativity. Before long you can use the technique on a live, intractable problem. The solution will be a 'creative product' of value and maybe originality and you will boost your CQ in the process.

Force field analysis

This popular technique identifies the positive and negative factors or 'forces' at work in any problem. It is rather like listing pros and cons. In this case you list those helping you to achieve what you want (including to mitigate a problem) and those preventing or hindering you. There may be several of each, and the creativity is in thinking of factors you would not normally have thought of. The idea then is to maximize the positive forces and minimize the negative forces so that you reach an equilibrium you can live with. A negative force may be turned into an opportunity or redefined as a positive factor when seen from a different point of view.

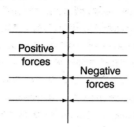

Another version is putting what you want or need (say in planning a project like a house move, or major work task) on one side and what might prevent you getting it on the other.

Yet another version is listing what you want as positives and what you don't want as negatives – for example, as applied to a career change or home relocation decision. By having to express these in words it helps to clarify your thoughts. By thinking of factors as forces you may see the problem more objectively as a trade-off of positive and negative. The more items you think of in all these cases, the more useful the technique will be.

How-to diagram

This is an example of various techniques that apply the 'question words', what, why, who, where, when and how. The benefit of the How? provocation is that you address a problem from a practical point of view – not just what to do but how to do it. That concentrates the mind in a particular way and, as the How To 'tree' progresses, brings you to the point where you have to do something simple like making a telephone call.

After each How To you ask another How To leading from the first but taking another angle. For example, How To get Val to stop parking in my place – How To get there earlier – How To not get bothered about little things – How To let down tyres in the dark, and so on. This technique usually does two things: 1) It redefines the problem – sometimes several times. By the time you have exhausted the How Tos and maybe started going round in circles you will have found the real problem, which is likely to be different to the 'presenting' problem, or the symptom. 2) By focusing on How To (rather than 'what' and 'why'), each answer will be *doable* with a specific action, or with a bit more thought.

If this example had gone down the route 'How To speak my mind and be assertive', you might have continued with

> *How To* get assertiveness training
> *How To* get sponsored
> *How To* find telephone number

and so on. Each How To gets nearer to a specific thing to do, even if it is just to get started. Even big, life-changing How Tos (like How To be assertive) lend themselves to the technique. You just need a few more How Tos and more creative insight.

Repetitive Why

This applies the Why question and is especially effective in redefining a problem. For example:

> **Problem:** Can't pay the bill.
> *Why?* overdrawn
> *Why?* paid holiday deposit
> *Why?* needed the break
> *Why?* mainly all the trouble with Chris
> *Why?* I suppose I was not spending enough time with
> him

and so on.

'Provocative' questioning techniques like Repetitive Why? will not necessarily solve the *presented* problem. But they often get things into better perspective, and identify a root problem that is more significant. A root problem might be the cause of *several* presented problems (in this case maybe headaches, other family problems, loss of promotion at work), so there are real long-term benefits in sorting out your life or your company (root problems tend to ignore personal and professional boundaries). It is also likely that the root or source problem is bigger than the one presented, which means on the face of it that you finish up worse off. However, that is not a very intelligent deduction, as not knowing you have a time bomb ticking away is a bigger problem than knowing it. Root problems used to be little ones – they got bigger because they remained below the surface for a long time.

You will get a similar result by rephrasing the questions and answers as follows:

> **Problem**: you've lost an important file.
> *Which was caused by*: untidy desk
> *Which was caused by*: not filing things last week
> *Which was caused by*: helping Charles out on his reconciliation
> *Which was caused by*: taking on too much work
> *Which was caused by*: not being assertive.

As with the How To diagram, it helps to get your stream of answers down on paper as this registers it better in your brain (which may want to defer or deny a thinking route). The diagram will also form a hierarchy, and any answer could take you down a different route with multiple destinations. You may even find more than one problem and of different kinds – for instance, one related to your work and another related to a family matter. In other cases branches of the Repetitive Why? tree tend to bring you back to the same, or a similar kind of problem.

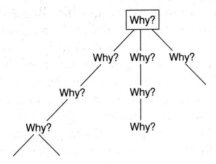

Typically it may boil down to assertiveness and not being able to say 'no', balance in different parts of your life, a particular relationship and so on. Recurring 'answers' are a good test that you have arrived at a real problem that is worth dealing with.

Points of view

Some techniques apply a checklist of questions that force you to think of an issue from different perspectives which usually provide new ideas and solutions. For example, you can:

- *chunk* up and down as we saw in the earlier technique;
- identify a *positive intention*, say on the part of a person involved;
- identify *another outcome* of the problem or situation, and imagine both positive and negative consequences;
- apply it *personally* asking whether this is to do with you as a person, and how specifically it goes against your values or beliefs ('it shouldn't be allowed');
- take a broad philosophical *'that's life'* approach';
- alter *timescales*, imagining how you will feel about the problem in a week, a month, a year, or how it would have affected you one year ago. Time is not significant in itself – we all perceive it differently – but the change in neural patterns this new viewpoint provokes makes all the difference;

- think of an *analogy*;
- see it from the viewpoint of somebody you know and respect.

Any of these perspectives may be enough to shake you out of a mental pattern that has helped to cause the *perception* of a problem. It is the sort of new perspective you get after a good night's sleep or after having a break from work or home responsibilities for a few days. It is simply a more purposeful and concentrated provocation of any angles that might help. Each point of view can be subjected to other techniques, such as brainstorming, to 'exploit' the angle more fully. Creative techniques do similar things and you can apply more than one to the same problem.

Reversal

Reversal techniques provoke lateral thinking by reversing a situation, statement or problem. The idea is, rather than considering partial, percentage changes as we normally do in a conscious, rational thinking mode, you turn the situation upside down or round 180 degrees and see what comes of it. The total disruption of familiar mental patterns helps to stimulate new associations and different perspectives on the same problem.

It can be as simple as reversing 'true' statements such as the items in a force field analysis or SWOT (strengths, weaknesses, opportunities, threats) analysis. For example, in a company a problem due to the fact that 'we are not market leader' would be subject to the reversal 'we are market leader'. You entertain new 'truths' for the purpose of disturbing old ones. As with other provocative techniques, you still have the divergent thinking to do yourself. In this case you would consider the implications of being market leader. There may be things you would be doing as market leader that you could actually be doing now. For instance, you could be doing some of the things that made somebody else market leader. Maybe you need to *think* 'market leader' just as the positive thinking books tell you to think yourself successful or rich. Reversal forces that thinking process. By writing down both problems and reversals your mind takes them on board and has 'permission' to do its creative job.

Reversing an issue is usually no more than a stimulus, just like a 'silly' idea (from someone else) in a brainstorming session. But even a spark of new meaning – or a way forward from a retractable situation – might be the mental break you need. Creativity is about seeing fundamentally different viewpoints, or opposites. Reversal does what a very creative person does – makes new meaning from existing disparate bits of meaning. Analogically, it looks at the 'forest' rather than the 'tree', and in doing so notices a few other things that help you to understand the tree better, plus things other than trees that may be useful.

Metaphor and analogy

The brain is *associative* and we can usually trace insights to the association of different unconnected ideas already in your mental database. A simple metaphor or simile is one example. You know what a rocket is and you know what Fred is like when he gets annoyed, so you have another way to look at or describe Fred. You know what a mist is like and you know the effect that Liz has on your mind when she goes on a bit, and by connecting the two concepts you have a synergistic, perhaps richer meaning in the mist metaphor. Likewise, a whole process can be analogous, such as comparing a growing tree with an organization or a distribution system with a spider building its web. In these cases a more complex relationship can produce many analogous relationships, any one of which could provide insight on a problem concerning an organization or logistics as the case may be. Processes from nature seem to be particularly useful and the supply is limitless, although synthetic processes like building a bridge or recycling cans can also be used. The less obvious or rational the link the better – your creative brain does the clever associative work.

Even random words can stimulate analogous thoughts, so you can pick words out of a dictionary. The ability to make connections is one feature of highly creative people and is good practice for anyone wishing to start thinking more divergently but in a risk-free situation. Think of any personal problem or issue, get your random word, relax, then say and write down whatever comes into your mind regarding your problem and the new thought. Say your problem is staying clear of an unwanted colleague ... hang on I'll get the dictionary ... I landed on 'oblique' – 'at an angle' or 'evasive'. It suggests not doing anything too direct but going in at an angle. Maybe take a different route to the canteen. Maybe look for a positive angle in which I can gain something, or use the situation as a learning experience and a test of character. Let what she says glance off me at an oblique angle so that it no longer affects me emotionally. Imagine that happening next time we meet. You can try another random word if the first doesn't look promising, but beware. This may be just the tendency not to want to disturb existing thought patterns and think in anything other than a rational, sensible way. Many great discoveries and inventions can be traced to the most outlandish ideas.

Graphical techniques

These comprise a whole range of techniques with graphical representations. 'Mind maps' are a common example today, but these date back to balloon diagrams, 'spoke and wheel' or 'hub and spoke' diagrams, and variations such as trees, hierarchies, cascade charts, flow charts, fish bones, and many more.

You can put words in circles (hence balloon diagrams), ovals or boxes as you wish – whatever seems most relaxing and productive. Some techniques do little more than change texts from the normal left to right, top to bottom orientation to a different form that resembles 'real' thinking more closely. That is fine, as the trick every time is to change familiar mental patterns, however you do it. Your unconscious brain does the difficult part.

Shapes and pictures have several advantages when stimulating divergent thinking. A tree-type structure allows unlimited growth – mirroring the fluidity, flexibility and elaboration of divergent thinking. These can go from left to right, which may add a time dimension, top to bottom or any way round. They allow for main ideas and also subsidiary, or consequential ideas. They allow space for new ideas in the form of another branch, spoke or twig as they occur to you. Diagrams with a central hub with spokes or sunbeams going out mean that there is no order or direction, so this promotes freer thinking. Used in note taking you can add extra spokes and, as with cascade or tree shapes, you can add sub-headings or incidental thoughts. An interesting idea can form the start of a new diagram on a new sheet of paper.

The right brain is particularly amenable to spatial layouts, and when combining it with words, as almost every graphical technique does, you have the symbolic and holistic dimensions together. The How To, Why Why and force field diagrams illustrate simple graphical techniques.

Techniques can double their value when you believe in your own creativity and get into the right state of mind. People have their favourite techniques that seem to work for them every time. I have found that reversal brings remarkable results in training programmes around the world and are adopted for many uses back in the workplace. It's best to try them all over a period. You will soon start to *think* intuitively in chunks, reversals, analogies and so on – with a purpose and creative product in view – just as an artist looks at the world in terms of colours, form and tone, with his or her next painting in mind. That's when you know your creativity has become a habit, and you are well up in the top CQ quartile. You can then expect frequent, special insights, exhilarating times of flow, and personal achievements one after another.

You can contact Harry Alder on
alder@creativityinc.fsnet.co.uk

Index